MEZZO-SOPRANO

Edited by Paolo Toscano

This edition is not authorized for sale in the EU or other European countries.

Assistant Editor: J. Mark Baker

Cover: *Il bacio* (The Kiss), 1859, Francesco Hayez

ISBN 978-0-634-04387-1

RICORDI

DISTRIBUTED BY

7777 W. BLUEMOUND RD. P.O. BOX 13819 MILWAUKEE, WI 53213

www.ricordi.com
www.halleonard.com

CONTENTS

INDEX

Aria Plots and Translations

ADRIANA LECOUVREUR

Music: Francesco Cilea. **Libretto:** Arturo Colautti, based on the play by Eugène Scribe and Ernest Legouvé. **First performance:** Teatro Lirico, Milan, 6 November 1902. **Setting:** Paris, 1730.

Acerba voluttà... O vagabonda stella

from Act II

Dramatic context: The Princess de Bouillion vies for the love of Maurice de Sax (Maurizio) with Adriana Lecouvreur, star actress of the Comédie-Française. In her soliloquy, she awaits Maurice's arrival for a tryst, wondering if he will come.

Acerba voluttà, dolce tortura,
lentissima agonia, rapida offesa,
vampa, gelo, tremor, smania, paura,
ad amoroso sen torna l'attesa!

Bitter pleasure, sweet torture,
slow agony, quick offense,
lashing heat, chills, trembling, desire, fear,
to a lover's heart anticipation returns!

Ogni eco, ogni ombra nella notte incesa
contro la impaziente alma congiura:
fra dubbiezza e desìo tutta sospesa,
l'eternità nell'attimo misura...

Every echo, every shadow in the burning night
plots against an impatient heart:
suspended between doubt and and desire,
a moment seems like eternity...

Verrà? M'oblia?
S'affretta? O pur si pente?
Ecco, egli giunge! No, del fiume è il verso,
misto al sospir d'un arbore dormente.

Will he come? Will he forget about me?
Will he hasten here? Or does he have regrets?
Here he comes! No, that's just the sound of the river,
mixed with the breeze through a willow.

O vagabonda stella d'Oriente,
non tramontar; sorridi all'universo,
e s'egli non mente, scorta il mio amor!

O wandering star of the East,
do not vanish; sparkle in the universe,
and if he is not deceiving me, then accompany my lover!

ALCINA

Music: George Frideric Handel. **Libretto:** Anonymous, adapted from Antonio Fanzaglia's libretto *L'Isola della Alcina*, after Ludovico Ariosto's epic poem *Orlando Furioso*. **First performance:** Covent Garden, London, 16 April 1735. **Setting:** Alcina's enchanted island.

Sta nell'Ircana pietrosa tana

from Act III

Dramatic context: The sorceress Alcina once again casts a spell on the knight Ruggiero in an attempt to make him love her. Her magic is ineffective, and Ruggiero declares his triumph.

Sta nell'Ircana pietrosa
tana tigre sdegnosa,
e incerta pende, se parte,
o attende il cacciator.

In its rocky Persian den
lurks the haughty tiger,
undecided whether to come out,
or lie in wait of the hunter.

Dal teso strale guardar si vuole;
ma poi la prole lascia in periglio.
Freme, e l'assale desìo di sangue,
pietà del figlio; poi vince amor.

Of the taughtly drawn arrow it must be wary;
but then it leaves its young in danger.
It roars, overcome by a thirst for blood,
yet pity for the cub; then love wins out.

L'AMICO FRITZ
(Friend Fritz)

Music: Pietro Mascagni. **Libretto:** Nicola Daspuro, based on the novel *L'Ami Fritz* by Émile Erckmann and Alexandre Chatrain. **First performance:** Teatro Costanzi, Rome, 31 October 1891. **Setting:** Alsace, late nineteenth century.

O pallida, che un giorno
from Act III

Dramatic context: Wealthy middle-aged landowner Fritz is secretly in love with Suzel, the pretty young daughter of one of his tenants, who returns his love. He becomes upset when he learns that she is to be married to another. To comfort him, the gypsy Beppe sings a song for Fritz, one written while he himself was suffering the pains of love.

O pallida, che un giorno mi guardasti,
in sogno tornami!
Una dolcezza tal mi procurasti,
che ancor ne ho l'estasi!
Oh! che chiedevi tu con gli occhi tuoi?
Ebbrezze, o lagrime?
Pallida, torna a me, dimmi che vuoi,
ch'io nulla negoti!
Nulla ti so negar, pallida mia,
t'ho dato l'anima.
E, se un tuo bacio dà la morte, sia!
Oh! vieni, baciami!

O pale spirit, who one day gazed upon me,
return to me in my dreams!
Such a sweet feeling you instilled in me
that I still feel the ecstasy!
Oh! what were you seeking with your gaze?
Rapture, or tears?
Pale image, return to me, tell me what you desire;
nothing will I refuse you.
Nothing could I refuse you, my pale spirit;
I have given you my soul.
And, if a kiss from you means death, so be it!
Oh! come, kiss me!

ANNA BOLENA
(Anne Boleyn)

Music: Gaetano Donizetti. **Libretto:** Felice Romani, after *Enrico VIII, ossia Anna Bolena* by Ippolito Pindemonte, and *Anna Bolena* by Alessandro Pepoli. **First performance:** Teatro Carcano, Milan, 20 December 1830. **Setting:** Windsor Castle, 1536.

È sgombro il loco… Ah! parea che per incanto
from Act I, scene 9 (now usually Act II, scene 1)

Dramatic context: Henry VIII has fallen in love with Giovanna Seymour (Jane Seymour), the lady-in-waiting to his wife and queen Anna Bolena (Anne Boleyn). In a hallway leading to Anna's private apartments, her page Smeton gazes longingly at a miniature of the Queen, kissing her portrait and singing of his love for her.

È sgombro il loco… Ai loro uffici intente
stansi altrove le ancelle… e dove alcuna
me qui vedesse, ella pur sa che in quelle
più recondite stanze, anco talvolta
ai privati concenti Anna m'invita.
Questa da me rapita
cara immagine sua, ripôr degg'io
pria che si scopra l'ardimento mio.
Un bacio, un bacio ancora,
adorate sembianze… Addio, beltade
che sul mio cor posavi,
e col mio core palpitar sembravi.

Ah! parea che per incanto
rispondessi al mio soffrire;
che ogni stilla del mio pianto
risvegliasse un tuo sospir.
A tal vista il core audace,
pien di speme e di desir,
ti scopria l'ardor vorace
che non oso a lei scoprir.

The place is deserted... Busy with their duties,
elsewhere are the handmaidens... and should one of them
spy me here, she would well know that in those
more secluded rooms, even sometimes
to private concerts Anna invites me.
This, which I took,
this dear image of her, I must replace
before my passion is discovered.
A kiss, yet another kiss,
beloved portrait... Goodbye, beauty
which rested next to my heart,
and with my heart seemed to beat as well.

Ah! it seemed as though by enchantment
you responded to my suffering;
that every teardrop I shed
awakened a sigh in you.
At that sight, a bold heart,
full of hope and desire,
would have revealed its consuming passion,
which I dare not reveal to her.

ARIODANTE

Music: George Frideric Handel. **Libretto:** Based on Antonio Salvi's *Ginevra, Principessa di Scozia*, after Ludovico Ariosto's epic poem *Orlando Furioso*. **First performance:** Covent Garden, London, 8 January 1735. **Setting:** Scotland, medieval times.

Dopo notte
from Act III

Dramatic context: Polinesso, Duke of Albany, plots to gain the throne of Scotland by discrediting the princess Ginevra in the eyes of Ariodante, who loves her. Polinesso is struck down in a duel with Lurcanio, but before he dies he confesses that he lied regarding Ginevra's infidelity to Ariodante. The death sentence which had been imposed on Ginevra is lifted. Ariodante rejoices.

Dopo notte, atra e funesta,
splende in ciel più vago il sole,
e di gioia empie la terra.

Mentre in orrida tempesta
il mio legno è quasi assorto,
giunge in porto, e 'l lido afferra.

After a sinister and dreadful night,
the sun shines more beautifully in the sky,
and fills the earth with joy.

Though in a fierce tempest
my ship was almost swallowed up,
it has reached port, and seizes the shore.

L'ARLESIANA
(The Girl from Arles)

Music: Francesco Cilea. **Libretto:** Leopoldo Marenco, based on the play *L'Arlésienne* by Alphonse Daudet. **First performance:** Teatro Lirico, Milan, 27 November 1897. **Setting:** Provence, nineteenth century.

Esser madre è un inferno
from Act III

Dramatic context: Federico is in love with a girl from Arles, but his mother Rosa Mamai and her godchild Vivetta, who loves him, show Federico letters proving the girl has been the mistress of Metifio, the stablehand. Though Federico consents to marry Vivetta, his passion for the Arlesian girl still burns; he attacks Metifio with a sledgehammer. Overwhelmed with all that has happened, Rosa Mamai offers a prayer that she will be strong to endure the suffering her son has caused her.

Esser madre è un inferno.
Ho dolorato fino quasi a morirne
il dì che venne alla luce.
Signor, tu che m'hai vista
alla sua cuna in quelle paurose
notti della sua infanzia... e tu lo sai
che te l'ho disputato ora per ora,
con la fronte dimessa al pavimento,
e con le palme aperte, in te converse,
invocando il tuo nome! Io da quei giorni
non ebbi requie più. Sai che gli ho dato
a brani a brani l'anima per farne
un uom che fosse onesto e forte, amore
e orgoglio mio. Io t'ho pregato tanto,
ma sempre in vano!
Sai che, se muor, né un'ora
gli sopravvivo, e morirò dannata!
Signor! tu che hai voluto
vane le preci mie insino ad ora
e vedermi piangente e dolorosa,
rammentati, Signor, la madre tua,
ai piedi della croce prosternata!...
Anch'io, Signor, son madre desolata.
Per pietà, veglia sulla vita sua,
per pietà, Signor!

To be a mother is misery.
I suffered almost to death
the day he was born.
Lord, you who saw me
beside his crib those frightening
nights of his infancy... and you know
I fought with you over him hour after hour,
with my forehead lowered to the floor,
with my palms open toward you in prayer,
invoking your name! After those days
I have never again had peace. You know that I gave,
bit by bit, my soul, to make of him
a man who would be honest and strong, my love
and my pride. I prayed to you often,
but always in vain!
You know that, should he die, not an hour
would I survive him, and I would die miserable!
Lord! you who have rendered
vain my prayers until now,
and have watched me weeping and suffering,
remember, Lord, your own mother
at the foot of the cross prostrate!...
I too, Lord, am a mother in distress.
I beg you, keep watch over his life,
I beg you, Lord!

BAJAZET
(ossia Tamerlano)
(Bajazet, or Tamerlane)

Music: Pastiche compiled by Antonio Vivaldi from several composers; this aria is now attributed to Geminiano Giacomelli (*c*1692-1740). **Libretto:** Agostin Piovene. **First performance:** Filarmonico, Verona, Carnival 1735.

Sposa son disprezzata
from Act II

Sposa son disprezzata,
fida son oltraggiata;
cieli che feci mai?

As a wife I am scorned;
in my loyalty I am insulted;
heavens, whatever did I do?

E pur egli è il mio cor,
il mio sposo, il mio amor,
la mia speranza.

And yet he is my heart,
my husband, my love,
my hope.

L'amo, ma egli è infedel;
spero, ma egli è crudel;
morir mi lascierai?

I love him, but he is unfaithful;
I am trusting, but he is cruel;
will you let me die?

O Dio, manca il valor e la costanza?

O God, what has become of honor and faithfulness?

UN BALLO IN MASCHERA
(A Masked Ball)

Music: Giuseppe Verdi. **Libretto:** Antonio Somma, after Eugène Scribe's libretto for Daniel-François-Esprit Auber's opera *Gustave III, ou Le Bal Masqué*, based on the assasination of Gustave III of Sweden at a masked ball in 1792. **First performance:** Teatro Apollo, Rome, 17 February 1859. **Setting:** The opera was originally planned to follow the *Gustave III* setting in late eighteenth century Sweden, but because of censorship the king was changed to a governor in Boston.

Re dell'abisso, affrettati
from Act I, scene 2

Dramatic context: At night in the hut of the fortune-teller Ulrica, a small crowd is present. As various private intrigues unfold, Ulrica begins her incantation.

Re dell'abisso, affrettati,
precipita per l'etra,
senza libar la folgore
il tetto mio penètra.
Omai tre volte l'upupa
dall'alto sospirò;
la salamandra ignivora
tre volte sibilò,
e delle tombe il gemito
tre volte a me parlò!

King of the depths, hasten;
plunge through the air;
without launching a lightning bolt
pierce my roof.
Already thrice the hoopoe
from on high has called;
the fire-eating lizard
thrice has hissed,
and from the tombs the moaning whisper
thrice has spoken to me!

È lui, è lui! ne' palpiti
come risento adesso
la voluttà riardere
del suo tremendo amplesso!
La face del futuro
nella sinistra egli ha.
M'arrise al mio scongiuro,
rifolgorar la fa:
nulla, piu nulla ascondersi
al guardo mio potrà!

It is he! In my trembling
how I now feel
the sensuousness burst aflame
from his tremendous embrace!
The torch of the future
he holds in his left hand.
He smiled upon my entreaty,
and relights it:
nothing, nothing more can hide
from my gaze!

Silenzio, silenzio!

Silence, silence!

IL BARBIERE DI SIVIGLIA

(The Barber of Seville)

Music: Gioachino Rossini, originally titled *Almaviva, ossia L'inutile precauzione* (Almaviva, or The Useless Precaution). **Libretto:** Cesare Sterbini, based on *Le Barbier de Séville*, a play by Pierre-Auguste Caron de Beaumarchais and the libretto for Giovanni Paisiello's *Il barbiere di Siviglia*. **First performance:** Teatro Argentina, Rome, 20 February 1816. **Setting:** Seville, eighteenth century.

Una voce poco fa

from Act I, scene 5

Dramatic context: Old Dr. Bartolo plans to marry his beautiful young ward Rosina. She, however, is in love with a student named Lindoro, who is actually the young Count Almaviva, incognito. He has serenaded her, and they have exchanged letters. Now, having read Lindoro's latest missive, Rosina resolves to thwart Bartolo's plans and follow the dictates of her own heart.

Una voce poco fa
qui nel cor mi risuonò;
il mio cor ferito è gia,
e Lindor fu che il piagò.
Sì, Lindoro mio sarà,
lo giurai, la vincerò.
Il tutor ricuserà,
io l'ingegno aguzzerò,
alla fin s'accheterà
e contenta io resterò.
Sì, Lindoro mio sarà,
lo giurai, la vincerò.
Io sono docile, son rispettosa,
sono ubbidiente, dolce, amorosa;
mi lascio reggere, mi fo guidar.
Ma se mi toccano
dov'è il mio debole,
sarò una vipera,
e cento trappole
prima di cedere
farò giocar.

A voice a moment ago
here in my heart echoed;
my heart is already wounded,
and it was Lindoro who pierced it.
Yes, Lindoro will be mine;
I made an oath, I shall prevail.
The tutor will object;
I'll sharpen my wit.
In the end he'll relent,
and happy I'll remain.
Yes, Lindoro will be mine;
I made an oath, I shall prevail.
I am docile, I'm respectful,
I'm obedient, sweet, and loving;
I submit to rule, I trust in guidance.
But if they dare touch me
where my weak spot is,
I can be a viper,
and a hundred traps
before giving up
I'll set.

I CAPULETI E I MONTECCHI

(The Capulets and the Montagues)

Music: Vincenzo Bellini. **Libretto:** Felice Romani, based on his libretto for Nicola Vaccai's *Giulietta e Romeo*, in turn based on Luigi Scevola's tragedy of the same name. **First performance:** Teatro La Fenice, Venice, 11 March 1830. **Setting:** Verona, thirteenth century.

Se Romeo t'uccise un figlio

from Act I

Dramatic context: Romeo has come, incognito, to the Capulets' palace to plead his case to Capellio, Giulietta's father. He offers to make peace by marrying Giulietta, thus joining two families who have feuded for many years. Capellio refuses, having betrothed Giulietta to Tebaldo. Capellio also believes Romeo has killed his son. If he did kill him, Romeo responds, only fate is to blame. If he is allowed to marry Giulietta, Capellio will have another son in him.

Se Romeo t'uccise un figlio,
in battatglia a lui diè morte:
incolpar ne dêi la sorte;
ei ne pianse, e piange ancor.
Deh! ti placa, e un altro figlio
troverai nel mio signor.

La tremenda ultrice spada
a brandir Romeo s'appresta,
e qual folgore funesta,
mille morti apporterà.

Ma v'accusi al ciel irato
tanto sangue invan versato;
e su voi ricada il sangue
che alla patria costerà.

If Romeo killed your son,
if in battle he struck him dead,
you must blame fate;
he wept over it, and weeps still.
Ah! assuage your anger, and another son
you will find in my lord.

The terrible vengeful sword
to brandish Romeo readies,
and like a deadly bolt of lightning,
a thousand deaths will it bring.

But your blame it will be before the wrath of heaven
for so much blood shed in vain;
and upon you will flow the blood
that it will have cost our homeland.

LA CENERENTOLA

(ossia La Bontà in Trionfo)
(Cinderella, or The Triumph of Goodness)

Music: Gioachino Rossini. **Libretto:** Jacopo Ferretti, after Charles Perrault's *Cendrillon* and probably both Charles-Guillaume Étienne's libretto for Niccolò Isouard's *Cendrillon* and the libretto for Stefano Pavesi's *Agatina*; also after the fairy tale. **First performance:** Teatro Valle, Rome, 25 January 1817. **Setting:** Don Magnifico's mansion and the court of Don Ramiro, time unspecified [probably eighteenth century].

Nacqui all'affano e al pianto... Non più mesta

from Act II

Dramatic context: The final scene of the opera takes place in the throne room of Prince Ramiro's palace. Angelina (Cenerentola) gathers her wedding guests around her following her marriage to the Prince. She absolves all who have been unkind to her, including her father and two stepsisters.

Nacqui all'affanno e al pianto. Soffrì tacendo il core; ma per soave incanto, dell'età mia nel fiore, come un baleno rapido la sorte mia cangiò.	*I was born to woe and weeping. My heart suffered in silence; but through a sweet enchantment, in the flower of my youth, like a flash of lightening my luck changed.*
No, no; tergete il cigilo. Perché tremar, perché? A questo sen volate; figlia, sorella, amica, tutto trovate in me.	*No, no; wipe your tears. Why do you tremble, why? Rush to this breast; a daughter, a sister, a friend: all that you will find in me.*
Non più mesta accanto al fuoco starò sola a gorgheggiar. Ah, fu un lampo, un sogno, un gioco il mio lungo palpitar.	*No longer sad by the fireplace will I remain singing all alone. Ah, only an instant, a dream, a jest was my long anguish.*

LA CLEMENZA DI TITO

(The Clemency of Titus)

Music: Wolfgang Amadeus Mozart. **Libretto:** Caterino Mazzolà, adapted from a libretto by Pietro Metastasio. **First performance:** National Theatre, Prague, 6 September 1791. **Setting:** Rome, *c*80 A.D.

Parto, ma tu, ben mio

from Act I

Dramatic context: Vitellia is so enraged with the Emperor Tito for slighting her by choosing to marry Berenice that she decides to lead a conspiracy against him. She urges the young patrician Sesto, who is madly in love with her, to assasinate Tito. Sesto, reluctant to betray his friend Tito, is finally coerced by Vitellia's promises of love. As he departs on his mission, he tells Vitellia that he will do whatever it takes to please her.

Parto, ma tu, ben mio, meco ritorna in pace; sarò qual più ti piace, quel che vorrai farò.	*I leave, but you, my beloved, will return to me in peace; I will be what most pleases you; what you want, I'll do.*
Guardami e tutto oblio, e a vendicarti io volo; a questo sguardo solo da me si penserà.	*Look at me and I'll forget everything, and I'll rush to avenge you; give only a glance and the deed by me will be done.*
Ah, qual poter, oh Dèi! donaste alla beltà.	*Ah, what power, oh Gods! did you bestow to beauty.*

Torna di Tito a lato

from Act II

Dramatic context: Acting on Vitellia's petition that he kill the Emperor Tito, Sesto has set fire to the city and has killed the wrong man. Sesto's friend Annio advises him to return to Tito, confess his wrongdoing, and offer proof of his faithfulness.

Torna di Tito a lato:
torna, e l'error passato
con replicate emenda
prove di fedeltà.

Return to Tito's side:
return, and the past error
you can amend with repeated
proof of your trustworthiness.

L'acerbo tuo dolore
è segno manifesto
che di virtù nel core
l'immagine ti sta.

Your bitter pain
is a clear sign
that with virtue in your heart
do you most befittingly seem to be.

Deh, per questo istante solo

from Act II

Dramatic context: Before signing Sesto's death warrant, the Emperor Tito summons his friend to court, hoping to uncover a reason to pardon him. Sesto refuses to disclose Vitellia's role in the conspiracy because Tito has agreed to marry her. Sesto tells the Emperor that his agony over having betrayed him is a fate worse than death itself.

Deh, per questo istante solo
ti ricorda il primo amor,
ché morir mi fa di duolo
il tuo sdegno, il tuo rigor.

Ah, for this moment only
remember your first love,
for it kills me, the pain
of your contempt, your severity.

Di pietade indegno è vero,
sol spirar io deggio orror.
Pur saresti men severo
se vedessi questo cor.

I am unworthy of mercy, it is true;
I should only die; what horror.
Yet you would be less severe
if you could see this heart.

Disperato vado a morte;
ma il morir non mi spaventa.
Il pensiero mi tormenta
che fui teco un traditor!

In despair I go to die;
but dying does not frighten me.
The thought that torments me is
that I was a traitor to you!

(Tanto affanno soffre un core,
né si more di dolor!)

(Great anguish a heart may suffer,
yet one does not die of the pain!)

COSÌ FAN TUTTE

(ossia La Scuola degli Amanti)
(Women Are Like That, or The School for Lovers)

Music: Wolfgang Amadeus Mozart. **Libretto:** Lorenzo da Ponte. **First performance:** Burgtheater, Vienna, 26 January 1790.
Setting: Naples, eighteenth century.

Smanie implacabili

from Act I, scene 3

Dramatic context: Dorabella thinks her soldier fiancé Ferrando has just gone off to war. Overwrought, she instructs the maid Despina to close the shutters, stating that she prefers to suffer in solitude until she finally dies of the pain of absent love.

Ah, scostati, paventa il tristo effetto
d'un disperato affetto!
Chiudi quelle finestre... odio la luce...
odio l'aria che spiro... odio me stessa...
Chi schernisce il mio duol... chi mi consola?
Deh fuggi, per pietà, lasciami sola.

Ah, go away, beware the sad effect
of a desperate emotion!
Close those windows... I hate the light...
I hate the air I breathe... I hate myself...
Who will make light of my pain... who will comfort me?
Ah, leave, for mercy's sake, leave me alone.

Smanie implacabili
che m'agitate,
dentro quest'anima
più non cessate
finché l'angoscia
mi fa morir.
Esempio misero
d'amor funesto
darò all'Eumenidi,
se viva resto,
col suono orribile
de' miei sospir!

O unquenchable desires
that trouble me,
within this soul
you must not cease
until the anguish
kills me.
A miserable example
of disastrous love
I will give to the Gods of Vengeance,
if I survive,
with the dreadful sound
of my sighs!

DON CARLO
(Don Carlos)

Music: Giuseppe Verdi. **Libretto:** Joseph Méry and Camille du Locle (in French), after Friedrich von Schiller's dramatic poem *Don Carlos, Infant von Spanien.* **First performance:** Opéra, Paris, 11 March 1867. **Setting:** Palace of King Philip II of Spain, Madrid, mid-sixteenth century.

O don fatale
from Act IV, scene 1

Dramatic context: Princess Eboli, lady-in-waiting to Elisabeth de Valois, Queen of Spain, has betrayed her mistress. She throws herself at Elisabeth's feet to confess two trangressions: that she has aroused Philip's suspicions because of her own jealousy, and that she herself has committed the adultery of which she suspected the Queen, having had an affair with the king. Elisabeth offers her the choice of being exiled or becoming a nun. Eboli laments the misery her fatal beauty has wrought.

O don fatale, o don crudel,
che in suo furor mi fece il cielo!
Tu che ci fai sì vane, altere,
ti maledico, o mia beltà!
Versar, versar sol posso il pianto,
speme non ho, soffrir dovrò!!
Il mio delitto è orribil tanto
che cancellar mai nol potrò!

O fateful gift, O cruel gift
that in its ire heaven gave me!
You that makes us so vain and proud,
I curse you, O my beauty!
I can shed, only shed tears,
I have no hope, I must suffer!
My crime is so terrible
that I can never erase it!

O mia Regina, io t'immolai
al folle error di questo cor.
Solo in un chiostro al mondo omai
dovrò celar il mio dolor!

O my Queen, I sacrificed you
to the foolish error of this heart.
Only in a cloister, from the world anymore
must I hide my suffering!

Oh ciel! E Carlo? a morte domani...
gran Dio! a morte andar vedrò!
Ah! Un dì mi resta, la speme m'arride!
Sia benedetto il ciel! Lo salverò!

Oh heaven! And Carlo? put to death tomorrow...
great God! to his death I'll see him go!
Ah! One day remains to me, hope smiles on me!
May heaven be blessed! I'll save him!

LA DONNA DEL LAGO
(The Lady of the Lake)

Music: Gioachino Rossini. **Libretto:** Andrea Leone Tottola, based on Sir Walter Scott's narrative poem "The Lady of the Lake." **First performance:** Teatro San Carlo, Naples, 24 October 1819. **Setting:** Scotland, first half of the sixteenth century.

Mura felici
from Act I, scene 7

Dramatic context: In a cottage on the shores of Lake Katrine, with the Ben Ledi mountains in the background, Malcolm is thinking of Elena, his beloved. Though she returns Malcolm's love, Elena's father has promised her hand in marriage to Roderigo. Alone, Malcolm sings of his hopes and fears.

Mura felici, ove il mio ben s'aggira!
Dopo più lune io vi reveggo. Ah! voi
più al guardo mio non siete
come lo foste un dì, ridenti, e liete!

Pleasant walls, where my beloved resides!
After many months I see you again. Ah! you
to my eyes no longer seem
as you did long ago, cheerful and pleasant!

Qui nacque, fra voi crebbe
l'innocente mio ardor: quanto soave
fra voi scorrea mia vita
al fianco di colei,
che respondea pietosa a' voti miei!

Here was born and raised
the innocent object of my passion; how sweetly
within you passed my life
with me beside her,
who responded mercifully to my vows!

Nemico nembo, or vi rattrista e agghiaccia
il povero mio cor! Mano crudele
a voi toglie, a me invola... oh, rio martoro!
la vostra abitatrice, il mio tesoro.

A hostile cloud now saddens you, and chills
my poor heart!A cruel hand
from you removes, from me abducts... oh, cruel torment!
your inhabitant, my treasure.

Elena, o tu che io chiamo!
Deh, vola a me un istante!
Tornami a dir "io t'amo."
Serbami la tua fé!

Elena, O you whom I call!
Ah, hurry to me for a moment!
Return to say "I love you."
Remain faithful to me!

E allor di te sicuro,
anima mia, lo giuro,
ti toglierò al più forte,
o morirò per te.
Grata a me fia la morte
s'Elena mia non è.

And thus, sure of your love,
my dear, I swear
that I'll seize you from the stronger man,
or I'll die for you.
Welcome to me be death
if Elena is not mine.

Oh, quante lagrime finor versai
lungi languendo da' tuoi bei rai!
Ogn'altro oggetto è a me funesto,
tutto è imperfetto, tutto detesto;
di luce il cielo, no, più non brilla,
più non sfavilla astro per me.
Cara! tu sola mi dai la calma,
tu rendi all'alma grata mercè!

Oh, how many tears I have thus far shed,
pining far away from your beautiful eyes!
Everything else seems dismal to me,
everything is imperfect, everything I detest;
the light in the sky, no, shines no more,
no star sparkles in the heavens for me.
Dear! you alone give me serenity;
you provide my soul with welcome comfort!

Tanti affetti in tal momento

from Act II

Dramatic context: The finale of the opera is set in a great room in Stirling Castle. Elena, the so-called "lady of the lake," loves Malcolm but has been promised to Rodrigo. She is also loved by Uberto (actually King James V in disguise) who pardons her father, a banished earl, and allows her to marry Malcolm.

Tanti affetti in tal momento
mi si fanno al core intorno,
che l'immenso mio contento
io non posso a te spiegar.

So much affection in this moment
surrounds my heart,
that my happiness is so great
I cannot describe it to you.

Deh! il silenzio sia loquace...
tutto dica un tronco accento...
Ah, signor! la bella pace
tu sapesti a me donar!

Ah! let the silence be eloquent...
let a brief word say it all...
Ah, lord! what wonderful peace
you have given me!

Fra il padre e fra l'amante
oh qual beato istante!
Ah! chi sperar potea
tanta felicità!

Between my father and my lover,
oh, what a blessed moment!
Ah! whoever could have hoped
for so much happiness!

EDGAR

Music: Giacomo Puccini. **Libretto:** Ferdinando Fontana, after Alfred de Musset's verse drama *La Coupe et les Lèvres.* **First performance:** Teatro alla Scala, Milan, 21 April 1889. **Setting:** Flanders, 1302.

Tu il cuor mi strazi

from Act I

Dramatic context: Tigrana, a seductive Moorish girl, has just come out of a tavern. She seats herself atop a table in the main square of the village. Accompanying herself on a lute-like instrument, she begins a provocative song.

"Tu il cuor mi strazi. Io muoio!
Che feci a te, crudel?"
belava all'avvoltoio
nell'agonia l'agnel…
Agnellin, fai pietà!

"You tear apart my heart. I am dying!
What did I do to you, cruel one?"
bleated to the vulture
the lamb in agony…
Little lamb, how pitiful you are!

Sia per voi l'orazion,
è per me la canzon!
Vo' cantar, vo' trillar!
Chi non vuole ascoltar
torni in chiesa a pregar!

What for you is a prayer,
for me is a song!
I want to sing, I want to warble!
Whoever does not want to listen
may return to church to pray!

L'ira vostra o il perdon
io del par sprezzerò!
L'abborita canzon, ah! cantero.

Your anger and pardon
both I disdain!
The song you all abhor, ah! I will sing.

LA FAVORITA
(The Favorite)

Music: Gaetano Donizetti. **Libretto:** Alphonse Royer and Gustave Vaëz, after Baculard d'Arnaud's drama *Le Comte de Comminges;* additions by Eugène Scribe, based in part on his libretto for Donizetti's *L'Ange de Nisida.* The opera was originally sung in French (*La Favorite*), but performance in Italian has long been standard. **First performance:** Opéra, Paris, 2 December 1840. **Setting:** Spain; 1340; a salon in the palace of the Alcazar.

O mio Fernando
from Act III, scene 4

Dramatic context: Leonora is in love with Fernando, who returns her affection. Fernando, a monastic novice turned Spanish army officer, is granted a reward by the king for his bravery on the battlefield. Unaware that Leonora is the king's mistress, Fernando asks for her hand in marriage, and the monach finds it prudent to grant it. Leonora will sacrifice her own happiness to ensure Fernando's, and resolves to let him know the truth.

Fia dunque vero, oh ciel? desso… Fernando!
lo sposo di Leonora!
Tutto mel dice,
e dubbia è l'alma ancora
all'inattesa gioia! Oh Dio! Sposarlo?
Oh, mia vergogna e strema! In dote al prode
recar il disonor—no, mai; dovesse
esecrarmi, fuggir, saprà in brev'ora
chi sia la donna che cotanto adora.

Is it thus true, oh heaven? here… Fernando!
husband to Leonora!
Everything confirms it to me,
yet doubtful still remains my spirit
at this unexpected joy! Oh God! Marry him?
Oh, my immense shame! As a dowry to the hero
to bring dishonor—no, never; even if he should
curse me for it, I must run away; he'll know soon enough
who the woman is he so adores.

O mio Fernando! Della terra il trono
a possederti avria donato il cor;
ma puro l'amor mio come il perdono,
dannato, ahi lassa! è a disperato orror.
Il ver fia noto, e in tuo dispregio estremo
la pena avrommi che maggior si de';
se il giusto tuo disdegno allor fia scemo,
piombi, gran Dio, la folgor tua su me.

Oh, my Fernando! Of this earth even a throne,
to have you,my heart would have given;
but my love, pure as pardon itself,
is condemned, alas! to desperate loathing.
The truth will be known, and in your extreme contempt
my punishment will be the greatest possible;
if your righteous disdain would wane,
launch, great God, a lightening bolt upon me.

Su, crudeli, e chi v'arresta?
Scritto è in cielo il mio dolor!
Su, venite, ell' è una festa,
sparsa l'ara sia di fior.
Già la tomba a me s'appresta;
ricoperta in negro vel
sia la trista fidanzata
che reietta, disperata,
non avrà perdono in ciel.

Onward, cruel ones, and who would stop you?
Ordained in heaven is my suffering!
Come on then, there is a celebration;
let the altar be covered with flowers.
Already the tomb is ready for me;
covered by a black veil
may the unhappy betrothed be
who, outcast, desperate,
will have no pardon from heaven.

Maledetta, disperata,
non avrà perdono in ciel.

Cursed, desperate,
she will have no pardon from heaven.

LA FORZA DEL DESTINO

(The Force of Destiny)

Music: Giuseppe Verdi. **Libretto:** Francesco Maria Piave, based on the Spanish drama *Don Alvaro, o La Fuerza del Sino* by Angel de Saavedra, Duke of Rivas. **First performance:** Imperial Theatre, St. Petersburg, 10 November 1862. **Setting:** Spain, mid-eighteenth century.

Al suon del tamburo

from Act II, scene 1

Dramatic context: In the inn at the village of Hornachuelos, a rich array of folk is gathered. Various town fathers, servants, muleteers, and a mysterious student sing and dance until the meal is announced. Preziosilla, a gypsy, arrives to tell the assembled that war has broken out and that they should make haste to Italy to fight the Germans. She sings a song extoling the delights of war, then tells the fortunes of those present, informing the "Studente" (Don Carlo incognito) in passing that his disguise does not fool her.

Al suon del tamburo,
al brio del corsiero,
al nugolo azzuro
del bronzo guerrier;
dei campi al susurro
s'esalta il pensier!

At the sound of the drum,
at the spirit of the charger,
at the bluish smoke
of the cannon;
at the buzz of the encampment
the mind exhalts!

È bella la guerra!
Evviva la guerra!

War is wonderful!
Hurray for war!

È solo obliato
da vile chi muore;
al bravo soldato,
al vero valor
è premio serbato
di gloria, d'onor!

Forgotten only
as a coward will be he who dies;
to the brave soldier,
to true valor
the prize offered
is glory and honor!

Se vieni, fratello,
sarai caporale;
e tu colonnello,
e tu generale.
Il dio furfantello
dall'arco immortale
farà di cappello
al bravo uffizial!

If you join, brother,
you'll be a corporal;
and you a colonel,
and you a general.
The rascally god
with the immortal bow
will salute
the good officer!

GIULIO CESARE

(Julius Caesar)

Music: George Frideric Handel. **Libretto:** Nicola Haym, adapted from Giacomo Francesco Bussani. **First performance:** King's Theatre, London, 20 February 1724. **Setting:** Alexandria, Egypt, 48 B.C.

Presti omai

from Act I

Dramatic Context: Julius Caesar has triumphed over his rival Pompey at Pharsalus. On a broad plain by the Nile River, a chorus of Egyptians greets the victorious Roman legions. Caesar himself enters, demanding a tribute of palm leaves, the symbol of victory.

Presti omai l'Egizia terra
le sue palme al vincitor!

Offer at last, of the land of Egypt,
her victory palms to the conqueror!

IDOMENEO
(Re di Creta)
(Idomeneo, King of Crete)

Music: Wolfgang Amadeus Mozart. **Libretto:** Abbé Gianbattista Varesco, after Antoine Danchet's libretto for Antoine Campra's opera *Idomenée;* also based on an ancient legend. **First performance:** Hoftheatre, Munich, 29 January 1781. **Setting:** Port of Sidon on the island of Crete near the end of the Trojan War, *c*1200 B.C.

Il padre adorato
from Act I

Dramatic context: Idomeneo, King of Crete, was shipwrecked while returning home from the Trojan War. In exchange for his life, he made a vow with Neptune, promising to sacrifice the first living creature he should meet. Back on land, it is his son Idamante whom he sees. Horrified, he orders his son away from his presence, leaving Idamante devastated at his father's apparent disapproval.

Il padre adorato
ritrovo, e lo perdo.
Mi fugge, sdegnato,
fremendo d'orror.

My adored father
I recover, and then lose.
He avoids me, indignant,
trembling with horror.

Morire credei
di gioia e d'amore:
or, barbari Dei!
m'uccide il dolor.

I thought I would die
of joy and love;
now, cruel Gods!
I die from anguish.

L'INCORONAZIONE DI POPPEA
(The Coronation of Poppea)

Music: Claudio Monteverdi. **Libretto:** Giovanni Francesco Busenello, based on the *Annals* by first-century Roman historian Tacitus. **First performance:** Teatro Santi Giovanni e Paolo, Venice, 1642. **Setting:** Rome, during the rule of Nero, 65 A.D.

A dio, Roma
from Act III

Dramatic context: The Roman emperor Nero has divorced his wife Ottavia, having declared his mistress Poppea the new empress. Now banished from Rome, Ottavia bids the Eternal City a poignant farewell.

A dio, Roma... a dio, patria... amici, a dio! |

Farewell, Rome... farewell, homeland... friends, farewell!

Innocente da voi partir conviene:
vado a patir l'esilio in pianti amari,
passerò disperata i sordi mari.

Though innocent, I must depart from you:
an exile of sad tears awaits me,
sailing in desperation the unheeding sea.

L'aria, che d'ora in ora
riceverà i miei fiati,
li porterà, per nome del cor mio,
a veder, a baciar le patrie mura.
Ed io starò solinga
alternando le mosse ai pianti, ai passi,
insegnando pietade ai tronchi e ai sassi.

The breeze, which from time to time
shall receive my breath,
will carry it, in the name of my heart,
to behold and kiss my homeland's walls.
And I shall be alone,
alternately weeping and pacing back and forth,
teaching the trees and stones themselves
to be compassionate.

Remigate oggi mai, perverse genti!
Allontanatevi omai dagli amati lidi.
Ahi, sacrilego duolo,
tu m'interdici 'l pianto
quando lascio la patria,
né stillar una lagrima poss'io,
mentre dico a' parenti e a Roma: a dio!

Use your oars today as never before, perverse people!
Transport me far from these dear shores.
Ah, sacrilegious grief,
proscribe my weeping
as I depart my homeland;
nor may I shed a tear
as I say to my family and to Rome: farewell!

L'ITALIANA IN ALGERI

(The Italian Girl in Algiers)

Music: Gioachino Rossini. **Libretto:** Angelo Anelli, originally for Luigi Mosca's 1808 opera of the same title. **First performance:** Teatro San Benedetto, Venice, 22 May 1813. **Setting:** Algiers, *c*1800.

Cruda sorte! Amore tiranno!

from Act I, scene 4

Dramatic context: While roaming the Mediterranean Sea looking for her lost love Lindoro, the Italian lady Isabella is shipwrecked at Algiers. A band of the Bey Mustafa's pirates, led by captain Ali, seize the ship and its passengers, looking on with delight at having discovered so many additions to Mustafa's harem. Isabella, wise to the ways of handling all sorts of men, says she will not be afraid.

Cruda sorte! Amor tiranno!
Questo è il premio di mia fé:
non v'è orror, terror, né affanno
pari a quel ch'io provo in me.

Per te solo, o mio Lindoro,
io mi trovo in tal periglio.
Da chi spero, oh Dio! consiglio?
Chi conforto mi darà?

Qua ci vuol disinvoltura,
non più smanie, né paura:
di coraggio è tempo adesso,
or chi sono si vedrà.

Già so per pratica
qual sia l'effetto
d'un sguardo languido,
d'un sospiretto...
So a domar gli uomini
come si fa.

Sien dolci o ruvidi,
sien flemma o foco,
son tutti simili
a presso a poco...
Tutti la chiedono,
tutti la bramano
da vaga femmina
felicità.

Cruel fate! Tyrannical love!
This is the reward for my constancy:
there is no horror, terror, or affliction
equal to what I now feel.

For you alone, O my Lindoro,
I find myself in such danger.
From whom can I hope, O God! to obtain counsel?
Who will give me comfort?

In this case I need to keep a cool head,
no more nervousness or fear:
this is the time for courage,
now we'll see what I'm made of.

I already know by experience
what effect
a languid look,
a subtle sigh can have...
I know how to take control
over men.

Whether they be gentle or rough,
calm or excitable,
they are all the same
more or less...
They all ask,
they all yearn
from an enchanting woman
for happiness.

LINDA DI CHAMOUNIX

(Linda of Chamonix)

Music: Gaetano Donizetti. **Libretto:** Gaetano Rossi, after *La Grâce de Dieu* by Adolphe-Philippe d'Ennery and Gustave Lemoine. **First performance:** Kärtnertortheater, Vienna, 19 May 1842. **Setting:** Chamonix, a mountain village of Savoy, *c*1760 (during the reign of Louis XV).

Cari luoghi ov'io passai

from Act I

Dramatic context: In the bustle of early morning activity, a group of young people from the village are departing for Paris to work through the winter as chimney sweeps and servants. Among them is the village poet Pierotto, Linda's childhood friend, whom all beg to sing his latest song. He favors them with a premonitory sad tale.

Cari luoghi ov'io passai
i primi anni di mia vita,
v'abbandono, e chi sa mai
quando ancor vi rivedrò!
Poveretto, abbandonato,
senza affetto e senza aita,
de' miei giorni il più beato
sarà il dì che tornerò.

Beloved places where I spent
the early years of my life,
I leave you, and who knows
when I'll see you again!
Poor, abandoned,
without care and without assistance,
of my days the happiest
will be the day I return.

Per sua madre andò una figlia
miglior sorte a rintracciar.
Colle lagrime alle ciglia
le dolenti si abbracciâr.
Pensa a me, dicea la madre,
serba intatto il tuo candore;
nei cimenti dell'amore
volgi al Nume il tuo pregar.
Ei non puote a buona figlia
la sua grazia ricusar.

For her mother a daughter departed,
a better fate to find.
With tears in their eyes
the sad pair embraced.
Think of me, said the mother,
keep intact your purity;
in the temptations of love
turn to God with your prayer.
He will not, to a virtuous daughter,
refuse His help.

Que' consigli, ahi, troppo poco
la fanciulla rammentò.
Nel suo cor s'accese un foco
che la pace le involò.
La tradita allor ritorna,
cerca invan di madre un seno;
di rimorsi il cor ripieno
una tomba ritrovò.
Sulla tomba finché visse
quella mesta lagrimò.

That advice, ah, too briefly
the maiden bore in mind.
In her heart there ignited a flame
that gave her no peace.
The betrayed girl then returned,
and sought in vain her mother's breast;
with a heart filled with remorse
she found a tomb.
On that tomb, for as long as she lived,
that unhappy woman wept.

MAOMETTO II

Music: Gioachino Rossini. **Libretto:** Cesare della Valle, after his play *Anna Erizo.* **First performance:** Teatro San Carlo, Naples, 3 December 1820; revised for Paris as *Le Siège de Corinthe.* **Setting:** Negroponte, the Venetian colony in Greece, fifteenth century.

Giusto ciel, in tal periglio

from Act I, scene 3

Dramatic context: The city of Negroponte is besieged by the army of Muslim leader Maometto II. The enemy attack is announced by a cannon shot and a cry of alarm. The Venetian commanders grab their swords as they rush away. The Venetian girl Anna, trembling with fear, runs with the other women to kneel in prayer before the temple.

Giusto ciel, in tal periglio,
più consiglio,
più speranza
non m'avanza,
che piangendo,
che gemendo
implorar la tua pietà.

Righteous heaven, in such danger
no better wisdom,
no more hope
remains to me
than, crying
and moaning,
to implore your mercy.

LE NOZZE DI FIGARO

(The Marriage of Figaro)

Music: Wolfgang Amadeus Mozart. **Libretto:** Lorenzo da Ponte, based on *La Folle Journée, ou Le Mariage de Figaro,* a comedy by Pierre-Auguste Caron de Beaumarchais. **First performance:** Burgtheater, Vienna, 1 May 1786. **Setting:** Count Almaviva's château near Seville, eighteenth century.

Non so più

from Act I

Dramatic context: Cherubino, Count Almaviva's teenage page, is telling Susanna, the chambermaid to the Countess, of his sad plight. The Count has caught him embracing Barbarina, the gardener's daughter. Though his master has threatened to banish him from the palace, he forgets about his bad fortune when he sees Susanna holding a ribbon belonging to the Countess. Snatching it from her hand, he breathlessly explains that every woman excites his passion.

Non so più cosa son, cosa faccio,
or di foco, ora sono di ghiaccio,
ogni donna cangiar di colore,
ogni donna mi fa palpitar.
Solo ai nomi d'amor, di diletto,
mi si turba, mi s'altera il petto
e a parlare mi sforza d'amore
un desìo ch'io non posso spiegar.

I no longer know who I am, or what I'm doing,
now I'm aflame, the next moment frozen,
every woman changes my mood,
every woman makes my heart pound.
The mere mention of love, of pleasure,
upsets me, changes my heartbeat,
and in speaking of love there wells up within me
a desire that I cannot explain.

Parlo d'amor vegliando,
parlo d'amor sognando,
all'acqua, all'ombra, ai monti,
ai fiori, all'erbe, ai fonti,
all'eco, all'aria, ai venti,
che il suon de' vani accenti
portano via con sé.

I speak of love awake,
I speak of love dreaming,
to the water, to the shadows, to the mountains,
to the flowers, to the forests, to the springs,
to the echo, to the air, to the winds,
which take the sound of useless words
and carry them away with them.

E se non ho chi m'oda,
parlo d'amor con me.

And if I have no one to hear me,
I speak of love to myself.

ORFEO ED EURIDICE
(Orpheus and Euridice)

Music: Christoph Willibald von Gluck. **Libretto:** Ranieri de' Calzabigi. **First performance:** Burgtheater, Vienna, 5 October 1762. **Setting:** Greece, mythological times.

Addio, o miei sospiri
from Act I

Dramatic context: The musician Orfeo grieves for his beloved Euridice, who has been killed by a deadly snake. Zeus, seeing his distress, sends Amor to tell Orfeo that he may go down to Hades and bring Euridice back with him. However, he must not look upon her face until they are safely returned from the underworld. Exultant at this news, Orfeo says goodbye to his sighs and weeping and leaves for the underworld.

Addio, o miei sospiri,
han speme i miei desiri;
per lei soffrir vo' tutto,
ed ogni duol sfidar!

Goodbye, oh my sighs,
my desires have hope;
for her I will suffer anything,
and brave any pain!

Addio, o miei sospiri,
han speme i miei desiri;
per lei vo' tutto osare,
ed ogni duolo e periglio sfidar!

Goodbye, oh my sighs,
my desires have hope;
for her I will brave all,
and every pain I will brave!

Io vo da l'atre sponde
varcar di Stige l'onde,
e de l'orrendo Tartaro
le Furie superar,
tutti quei superar!

I'll go from the sinister banks
to navigate the waves of the Styx,
and of the horrible Tartarus
the Furies conquer,
I'll conquer them all!

ORLANDO FINTO PAZZO
(Orlando, the Feigned Lunatic)

Music: Antonio Vivaldi. **Libretto:** Grazio Braccioli. **First performance:** San Angelo, Venice, November 1714.

Anderò, volerò, griderò
from Act III

Dramatic context: Orgille vows to seek revenge on every heart that boasts of valor. The same aria appears as "Andrò, chi amerò dal profondo" in Vivaldi's *Orlando furioso.*

Anderò, volerò, griderò,
su la Senna, su il Tebro, su il Reno,
animando a battaglia, a vendetta
ogni cuore che vanti valor.

I'll go, I'll fly, I'll shout,
on the Siene, on the Tiber, on the Rhine,
rousing to battle and revenge
every heart that boasts of valor.

Empio duol che me serpi nel seno,
scaglia pur la fatale saetta,
a finire il mio acerbo dolor.

Cruel pain that creeps within my breast,
launch, if you will, the inevitable thunderbolt
that will end my bitter suffering.

OTELLO

Music: Gioachino Rossini. **Libretto:** Francesco Berio di Salsa, loosely based on William Shakespeare's *Othello.* **First performance:** Teatro del Fondo, Naples, 4 December 1816. **Setting:** Cyprus, late fifteenth century.

Assisa a piè d'un salice

from Act III, scene 1

Dramatic context: Due to her father's opposition to the match, Desdemona has secretly married Otello. When Desdemona's father arranges her betrothal to Rodrigo, the clandestine union is exposed. Iago encourages Otello's jealousy by showing him a letter written by Desdemona. Spurned by her husband, Desdemona sings the mournful "Willow Song," accompanying herself on the harp.

Assisa a piè d'un salice,
immersa nel dolore
gemea trafitta Isaura
dal più crudele amore;
l'aura fra i rami flebile
ne ripeteva il suon.

Seated at the foot of a willow,
absorbed in her pain,
Isaura lamented, stricken
by love most cruel;
the wind in the branches softly
repeated the sound.

I ruscelletti limpidi
ai caldi suoi sospiri
il mormorio mescevano
de' lor diversi giri;
l'aura fra i rami flebile
ne ripeteva il suon.

The clear brooks
with her passionate sighs
mingled the murmur
of their meandering;
the wind in the branches softly
repeated the sound.

Salce, d'amor delizia,
ombra pietosa appresta
(di mie sciagure immemore)
all'urna mia funesta,
né più ripeta l'aura
de' miei lamenti il suon.

Willow, the delight of love,
cast a merciful shadow
(forgetful of my troubles)
on my funeral urn,
and never again may the breeze repeat
the sound of my sorrow.

Ma stanca alfin di spargere
mesti sospiri e pianto,
morì l'afflitta vergine
ahi! di quel salce accanto!

But tired at last of shedding
melancholy sighs and tears,
the stricken virgin died
ah! beside that willow!

Morì... che duol! l'ingrato...
Ahimè! che il pianto proseguir non mi fa.

She died... what pain! the ingrate...
Alas! my tears will not let me continue.

Deh! calma, o ciel, nel sonno
per poco le mie pene;
fa' che l'amato bene
mi venga a consolar.

Ah! soothe, O heaven, in sleep,
however briefly, my suffering;
cause my beloved
to come to comfort me.

Se poi son vani i prieghi,
di mia breve urna in seno
di pianto venga almeno
il cenere a bagnar.

And if my prayers are in vain,
on my small urn, as token of his
tears may he come at least
to wet the ashes.

SEMIRAMIDE

Music: Gioachino Rossini. **Libretto:** Gaetano Rossi, after Voltaire's tragedy *Sémiramis.* **First performance:** Teatro La Fenice, Venice, 3 February 1823. **Setting:** Babylon, eighth century B.C.

Bel raggio lusinghier

from Act I, scene 1

Dramatic context: Surrounded by the ladies of her court in the hanging gardens of the palace, Semiramide expresses her joy that Arsace has returned. The Queen is in love with the young general and plans to marry him, hoping finally to resolve the problems which beset the kingdom. She does not realize that Arsace is actually her son.

Bel raggio lusinghier
di speme e di piacer
alfin per me brillò:
Arsace ritornò, sì, a me verrà.

Beautiful alluring beam
of hope and pleasure—
in the end, it shone for me:
Arsace returned; yes, he will come to me.

Quest'alma che sin'or
gemé, tremò, languì...
oh! come respirò!
Ogni mio duol sparì
dal cor, dal mio pensier
si dileguò il terror!

This heart which up to now
mourned, trembled, languished...
oh! how it sighed!
All pain vanished
from my heart; from my thoughts
the fear disappeared!

La calma a questo cor
Arsace renderà.
Arsace ritornò, quì a me verrà!

Peace to this heart
Arsace will bring.
Arsace returned, and will come here to me!

Dolce pensiero
di quell'istante,
a te sorride
l'amante cor.

O sweet thought
of that moment,
upon you smiles
this loving heart.

Come più caro,
dopo il tormento,
è il bel momento
di gioia e amor!

How much more precious,
after the anguish,
is the wonderful moment
of joy and love!

In sì barbara sciagura

from Act II, scene 4

Dramatic context: Arsace learns from the high priest Oroe that he is the son of Semiramide and the late king Nino, and is therefore heir to the throne of Babylon. Oroe tells Arsace that his mother Semiramide and her lover Prince Assur plotted to poison Nino in order to bring Assur to power. Both furious and sorrowful at this revelation, Arsace laments the death of his father and then swears vengeance. Filial love leads him to forgive his mother, but he declares that Assur must be punished.

In sì barbara sciagura,
m'apri tu le braccia almeno,
lascia a te ch'io versi in seno
il mio pianto, il mio dolor!
A quest'anima smarrita,
porgi tu conforto, aita.
Di mie pene al crudo eccesso,
langue oppresso in petto il cor.

In such cruel misfortune,
you, at least, open your arms to me,
let me spill on your breast
my tears, my pain!
To this lost soul
offer your comfort, your aid.
Of woes so terribly harsh
my heart languishes heavy in my breast.

Sì, vendetta! Porgi omai!
Sacro acciar del genitore,
tu ridesti il mio valore,
già di me maggior mi sento.
Sì, del ciel, nel fier cimento,
il voler si compierà!
Sì, l'empio cada!

Yes, revenge! Let it be done!
Sacred sword of my father,
you must restore my valor;
already I seem stronger.
Yes, in this difficult task, heaven's
wish will be done!
Yes, the wicked one shall fall!

Ah! ella è mia madre!
Al mio pianto forse il padre
perdonarle ancor vorrà.

Ah! she is my mother!
At my tears, perhaps my father
would nonetheless wish to forgive her.

Sì, vendicato
il genitore,
a lui svenato
il traditore,
pace quest'anima
sperar potrà.

Yes, when avenged be
my father,
severed be
the traitor's veins;
then peace this soul
can hope to find.

Ai dolci palpiti
di gioia e amore,
felice il core
ritornerà.
Al gran cimento m'affretto ardito;
meco l'Assiria
respirerà.

To the sweet pulse
of joy and love,
happily this heart
will return.
To the great challenge I rush boldly;
with me Assyria
will find relief.

TANCREDI

Music: Gioachino Rossini. **Libretto:** Gaetano Rossi, based on Voltaire's *Tancrède.* **First performance:** Teatro La Fenice, Venice, 6 February 1813. **Setting:** Syracuse on the island of Sicily, 1005 A.D.

Di tanti palpiti
from Act I, scene 5

Dramatic context: Tancredi returns to Syracuse, which has been besieged by the Saracens. Disembarking from his ship, he sings of his love for his native soil and longs to see Amenaide, his beloved. Tancredi is unaware that Amenaide has become engaged to Orbazzano during his absence.

Oh patria! dolce, e ingrata patria! alfine
a te ritorno! Io ti saluto, o cara
terra degli avi miei: ti bacio. È questo
per me giorno sereno:
comincia il cor a respirarmi in seno.

Amenaide! o mio pensier soave,
solo de' miei sospir, de' voti miei
celeste oggetto, io venni alfin: io voglio,
sfidando il mio destino, qualunque sia,
meritarti, o perir, anima mia.

Tu che accendi questo core,
tu che desti il valor mio,
alma gloria, dolce amore,
secondate il bel desìo,
cada un empio traditore,
coronate la mia fé.

Di tanti palpiti,
di tante pene,
da te mio bene,
spero mercé.
Mi rivedrai...
ti rivedrò...
ne' tuoi bei rai
mi pascerò.

Deliri, sospiri,
accenti, contenti!...
Sarà felice, il cor mel dice,
il mio destino vicino a te.

O homeland! sweet, yet ungrateful homeland! at last
I return to you! I greet you, O beloved
land of my forefathers: I kiss you. This is
a peaceful day for me:
my heart awakens in my breast.

Amenaide! O dear object of my thoughts,
my single source of yearning, of my prayers
their heavenly motive, at last I have come: I want,
notwithstanding my fate, whatever it may be,
to be worthy of you, or to die, my love.

You who rouse this heart,
you who inspire my courage,
proud spirit, sweet love,
sustain my splendid wish:
may a wicked traitor fall;
reward my faith.

Amidst so much anguish,
so much suffering,
from you, my beloved,
I hope to receive mercy.
You will see me again...
I will see you again...
Your radiant gaze
will nourish me.

Ecstasy, yearning,
tender words, contentment!...
Happy will be—my heart tells me so—
my destiny beside you.

IL TROVATORE
(The Troubador)

Music: Giuseppe Verdi. **Libretto:** Salvadore Cammarano (completed by Leone Emanuele Bardare after Cammarano's death in 1852), based on the Spanish play *El Trovador* by Antonio Garcia Gutiérrez. **First performance:** Teatro Apollo, Rome, 19 January 1853. **Setting:** Spain, fifteenth century; a gypsy camp in the mountains, early morning.

Stride la vampa
from Act II, scene 1

Dramatic context: The gypsies sing a rhythmic song as they work at their anvils by the fire. Their happy mood evaporates when the old gypsy Azucena tells the story of how her mother was burned at the stake for being a witch, while her false accusers screamed with delight.

Stride la vampa! la folla indomita
corre a quel foco, lieta in sembianza!
Urli di gioia intorno echeggiano;
cinta di sgherri donna s'avanza;
sinistra splende sui volti orribili
la tetra fiamma che s'alza al ciel!

The blaze roars! the wild crowd
rushes to that pyre, smiles on their faces!
Shouts of joy echo all around;
surrounded by thugs the woman advances;
a sinister glow reflects on those gruesome faces
from the funereal flame that shoots to the sky!

Stride la vampa! giunge la vittima
nero vestita, discinta e scalza;
grido feroce di morte levasi;
l'eco il ripete di balza in balza;
sinistra splende sui volti orribili
la tetra fiamma che s'alza al ciel!

The blaze roars! the victim arrives
dressed in black, half-stripped and barefoot;
a savage cry of death rises up;
the echo repeats again and again;
a sinister glow reflects on those gruesome faces
from the dismal flame that shoots to the sky!

Condotta ell'era in ceppi

from Act II, scene 1

Dramatic context: Continuing her story, Azucena tells Manrico the complete sequence of events that occurred at her mother's execution: As her mother was being burned at the stake, she cried out to Azucena to avenge her. Azucena took the baby son of the old Count di Luna, intending to throw him into the same fire in which her mother died. In her madness, though, Azucena mistakenly threw her own baby into the fire, then kept the Count's son for herself.

Condotta ell'era in ceppi al suo destin tremendo;
col figlio sulle braccia, io la seguia piangendo.
Infino ad essa un varco tentai, ma invano, aprirmi...
Invan tentò la misera fermarsi e benedirmi!

Ché, fra bestemmie oscene, pungendola coi ferri,
al rogo la cacciavano gli scellerati sgherri!
Allor, con tronco accento, "Mi vendica!" esclamò...
Quel detto un eco eterno in questo cor lasciò.

Il figlio giunsi a rapir del Conte;
lo trascinai qui meco...
le fiamme ardean già pronte.

Ei distruggeasi in pianto...
Io mi sentiva il core dilaniato, infranto!

Quand'ecco agli egri spirti,
come in un sogno, apparve
la vision ferale di spaventose larve!

Gli sgherri! ed il supplizio!...
la madre smorta in volto...
scalza, discinta!...
il grido, il noto grido ascolto...
"Mi vendica!"...
La mano convulsa tendo... stringo
la vittima... nel foco la traggo, la sospingo!...
Cessa il fatal delirio...
l'orrida scena fugge...
la fiamma sol divampa, e la sua preda strugge!
Pur volgo intorno il guardo, e innanzi a me vegg'io
dell'empio Conte il figlio!

Il figlio mio,
mio figlio avea bruciato!

Sul capo mio le chiome sento drizzarsi ancor!

She was led in chains to her terrible fate;
with the child in my arms, I followed her weeping.
I tried to break through to reach her, but in vain...
In vain the unhappy woman tried to stop and bless me!

For, with obscene curses, prodding her with their
weapons,
they pushed her toward the stake, those vile thugs!
Then, with a broken voice, "Avenge me!" she cried...
That phrase echoed forever within my heart.

The Count's child I succeeded in kidnapping;
I dragged him here with me...
the flames were already high.

He desperately was crying...
I felt my heart torn apart, broken!

When suddenly, to my suffering spirit,
as if in a dream, there appeared
the infernal vision of frightening phantoms!

The thugs! and the torture!...
my mother's pallid face...
barefoot, half stripped!...
the cry, the unforgotten cry I hear...
"Avenge me!"...
My trembling hand reaches out... I hold
the victim... I drag him to the fire, I push him in!...
The inexorable delirium ends...
the horrible scene disappears...
the fire alone blazes, and consumes its victim!
Yet I turn my gaze and see before me
the wicked Count's son!

My son,
my own son I had killed!

My hair rises again on my head at the thought!

O pallida, che un giorno

L'AMICO FRITZ

Pietro Mascagni
(1863-1945)

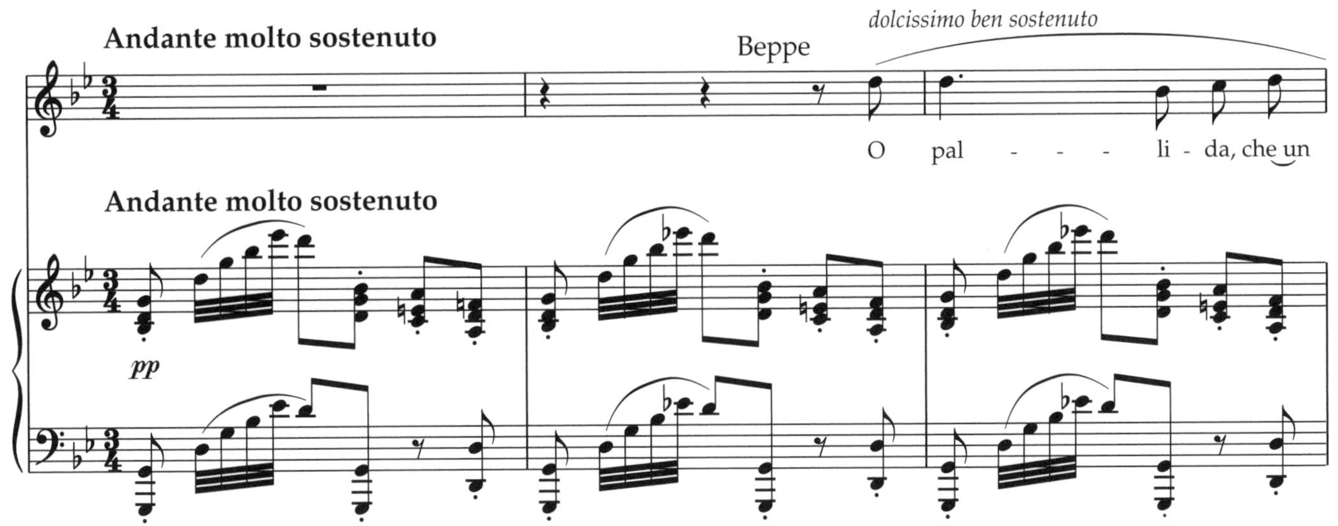

10
l'e - sta - si!
a tempo
Oh! che chie - de - vi
più f animato
rall.
p a tempo
12
tu con gli oc - chi tuo - - - i? Eb - brez - - - ze, o
f
rallentando
p subito
15
la - - gri - me? Pal - li - da, tor - na a me, dim - mi che
a tempo, con molta anima
più f a tempo, con molta anima
animando e sempre cresc.
18
vuo - - - i, ch'io nul - la ne - - - - - - go - ti!

Più mosso (♩ = 69)
Nul - la ti so ne - gar, pal - li - da mi - - - a, t'ho da - to
Più mosso (♩ = 69)
f
un poco rit.
rit.
l'a - - - - ni - ma. E, se un tuo ba - cio dà la mor - te, si - a!
p
rit. col canto
f rit.
ff ten. a piacere
lunga
Oh! vie - ni, vie - ni, ba - - - cia - mi!
8va
f col canto
mf a tempo
f
ff

Acerba voluttà... O vagabonda stella

ADRIANA LECOUVREUR

Francesco Cilea
(1866-1950)

20
ten.
u - - ra, ad a - mo - ro - so sen tor - na l'at -
f
dim.
25
Largo (♩ = 126)
te - - sa!
Largo (♩ = 126)
ff
pp e cupo
sf
30
f
Agitato (𝅗𝅥 = 84)
O - gni e - - co, o -
Agitato (𝅗𝅥 = 84)
p
sf
sf
34
gni om - bra nel - la not - - - te in - ce - sa
p

37
con - - tro la im-pa-zien - - - te al - - - ma con -
sf p
40
giu - - ra: fra dub - biez - za
p
43
e de - sì - o tut - ta so-spe - sa,
crescendo
47
l'e - ter-ni - tà nel - l'at-ti-mo mi - su - - - ra...
mf
ff

Con moto (♩ = 176)
52
pp leggerissimo
54
57
p
Ver - rà?
M'o - bli - a?
S'af -
poco crescendo
60
fret - ta?
O pur si
pen - - - te?

63
Ec-co, e - gli giun-ge!
No, del fiu - me è il
66
rall.
ten.
Sostenuto (♩ = 69)
ver - so, mi - sto al so - spir d'un ar - bo - re dor - men - te.
O va - ga -
Sostenuto (♩ = 69)
rall.
piú
70
bon - - - - da stel - la d'O - - - ri - en - - - - te,
73
non tra - mon - tar,
non tra - mon - tar;
rall.

77
sor - ri - - - - - di
p a tempo
79
al - l'u - - - - ni - ver - - - - - so,
81
f
e s'e - gli non men - te, scor - ta il mio a - mor!
f
ff
f
m.s.
85
m.s.

Sta nell'Ircana pietrosa tana

ALCINA

George Frideric Handel
(1685-1759)

a cura di J.M.B.

13
Ruggiero
Sta nel - l'Ir - ca - - na
tr
p
16
pie - tro - sa ta - - - na ti - gre sde - gno - - - sa,
18
e in - cer - ta pen - - - de, se par - te, o at - ten - de
20
il cac - cia - tor, ti - gre sde - gno -
f
p

23
26
sa,
29
in - cer - ta pen - de,
se par - te, o at - ten - de,
31
se par - te, o at - ten - de il cac - cia - tor, se

33
par - te, o at - ten - - - - - - - - de il
35
tr
cac - cia - tor.
f
38
Sta nel - l'Ir - ca - na
p
41
pie - tro - sa ta - na ti - gre sde - gno - sa, ti - gre sde - gno - sa,

44
e in-cer - ta pen - de,
se par-te, o at-ten - de
il cac-cia - tor,
47
ti - gre sde-gno
50
53

56
- - sa, in cer - ta pen - de, se par-te, o at-ten - de,
59
se par-te, o at-ten - - de il cac - - cia - - tor, se
61
par - te, o at - ten - - de il cac - cia - tor, se par - - - te, o at -
64
[rit.]
ten - - - de, in - cer - - ta pen - de, se par-te, o at-ten - de il
[rit.]

67
cac - - cia-tor.
f
[a tempo]
70
73
Fine
Dal
tr
Fine
76
te - so stra - le guar-dar si vuo - le; ma poi la pro - le
p

79
la-scia in pe - ri - glio. Fre - me, e l'as - sa - - - - - le
82
de - sìo di san - gue,
pie - tà del fi - glio;
poi vin - ce a - mor, poi
85
vin - ce a - mor. Fre - - - me, e l'as - sa - le
de - sìo di san - gue,
88
Adagio
D.C. al Fine
pie - tà del fi - glio;
poi vin - ce a - mor, poi vin - ce a - mor.
Adagio
D.C. al Fine

È sgombro il loco... Ah! parea che per incanto

ANNA BOLENA

Gaetano Donizetti
(1797-1848)

18
20
calando
Smeton
È sgom - bro il
f
22
lo - co... Ai lo-ro uf - fi - ci in - ten - te stan-si al-tro - ve le an-cel - le... e do-ve al -
25
cu-na me qui ve - des - se, el - la pur sa che in quel-le più re - con-di-te stan-ze, an - co tal -
p col canto

29
vol-ta ai pri-va - ti con - cen-ti An - na m'in - vi - ta. Que-sta da me ra -
p
33
lento
pi - ta ca-ra im-ma - gi-ne su - - - a, ri-pôr deg-g'i - o pria che si
p lento
36
Larghetto
sco-pra l'ar - di-men-to mi - o. Un ba - - - cio, un ba-cio an -
Larghetto
p
39
co - - - ra, a - do - ra - - - - te sem -

41
cresc. d'anima
bian - ze... Ad - di - - - - o, ad - dio, bel -
43
p
ta - - de che sul mio cor po - sa - vi, e col mio
46
a piacere
co - re pal - pi - tar sem - bra - vi, ad - - - - di -
col canto
Moderato
48
o.
Moderato
f
p

53
f
57
dolce
Ah! pa - re - a che per in - can - to ri - spon - des - si al mio sof -
fz
p
61
fri - re; che o - gni stil - la del mio pian - to ri - sve-glias - se un tuo so -
65
spir, ri - sve - glias - se un tuo so - spir. A tal
col canto

68
vi - sta il co - re au - da - ce, pien di spe - me e di de -
71
sir, ti sco - pri - a l'ar - dor vo - ra - ce che non
74
o - so a lei sco - prir. A tal vi - sta il co - re au -
p
77
accel. e rinf.
da - ce, pien di spe - me e di de - sir, ti sco -
p
accel. e rinf.

80
pri - a l'ar - dor vo - ra - ce che non o - so a lei sco -
p
83
prir, ti sco - pri - a l'ar-dor vo - ra - ce che non o - so a lei sco -
87
Poco più mosso
prir. Ad - dio, bel -
Poco più mosso
p
90
ta - de che sul
crescendo

93
cor ——— po - sa - vi, ad - dio, bel -
f
ff
96
ta - de, bel - ta - - - - de ad - di - - - -
99
I° Tempo
o. Ah! ——— Ah! pa - re - a che per in - can - to ri - spon -
I° Tempo
p
p
103
des - si al mio sof - fri - re; che o - gni stil - la del mio

106
pian - to ri - sve - glias - se un tuo so - spir, ri - sve -
109
glias - se un tuo so - spir. A tal vi - sta il co - re au -
col canto
112
da - ce, pien di spe - me e di de - sir, ti sco -
115
pri - a l'ar - dor vo - ra - ce che non o - so a lei sco -

118
p
accel. e rinf.
prir. A tal vi - sta il co - re au - da - ce, pien di
accel. e rinf.
121
p
spe - - me e di de - sir, ti sco - pri - - a l'ar - dor vo -
p
124
ra - ce che non o - so a lei sco - prir, ti sco -
127
3
3
pri - - a l'ar - dor vo - ra - ce che non o - so a lei sco -

130
Più mosso
prir, no, non o - so sco - prir, no, non
Più mosso
f
133
o - so sco - prir, non o - so sco -
ff
136
prir, non o - so sco - prir, no, no, no, no, non
139
o - so a lei sco - prir.

Sposa son disprezzata
BAJAZET

Geminiano Giacomelli
(c1692-1740)
(formerly attr. Antonio Vivaldi)

21
za - ta, fi - da son ol-trag-gia - ta; cie -
[f]
f
26
- li che fe-ci mai? Cie - - - li che fe-ci mai? E
[p]
[f]
[p]
p
f
p
31
pur e-gli è il mio cor, il mio spo - so, il mio a-mor, la mia spe-ran - -
[cresc.]
[cresc.]
36
- - - - - - - - - - - za.
[f]
tr
f
[dim.]

41
[p]
Spo - sa son di-sprez -
p
46
[f]
za - ta, fi - da son ol-trag-gia - ta; cie -
f
51
[p]
[f]
[p]
- li che fe - ci mai? Cie - - - li che fe - ci mai? E
p
f
p
56
pur e - gli è il mio cor, il mio spo - so, il mio a - mor, la mia spe -

[p]
ran
[p]
za,
la mia spe - ran
[cresc.]
[cresc.]
f
f
za.
[dim.]

Andante
[mf]
L'a - mo, ma e-gli è in-fe - del;
Andante
[p]
Fine
[mf]
[p]
[mf]
spe - ro, ma e - gli è cru - del;
[p]
mo -
[p]
[mf]
rir mi la - scie - rai? Mi la - scie - rai mo - rir? O Dio, man - ca il va -
[cresc.]
[mf]
[p]
[cresc.]
[mf]
lor, man - ca il va - lor e la co - stan - - - - - - za?
[p]
tr
D.C. al Fine
[p]
D.C. al Fine

Dopo notte
ARIODANTE

George Frideric Handel
(1685-1759)

a cura di J.M.B.

17
po not - te, a - tra e fu - ne - sta,
22
splen - de in ciel più va - - - - - -
26
- - - - - - go il so - le, e di
30
gio - - - - - - - - - - - - -

34
38
42
ia em pie la ter
46
ra, e di gio ia em-pie

50
tr
la ter - - ra.
tr
[f]
54
58
Do - - - po
not - te,
a - tra e fu -
[mp]
62
ne - sta,
splen - de in ciel più
va - - - - go il

66
so - le, do - - po not - te, a - tra e fu -
70
ne - sta, splen - - - - - - - -
74
- - - - - - - - - - de in ciel più va - go il
77
so - le, più va - - - - - - - -

80
go il
84
so - le,
e
di
gio - ia
em - pie la
88
ter - ra,
di
gio
91

94
97
ia em - pie la ter -
101
ra,
di gio - - -
104

108
[rit.]
- ia em - pie la ter - ra.
[rit.]
tr
[f a tempo]
113
117
121
124
Fine
Men - tre in or - - - ri - da tem -
Fine
p

128
pe - sta il mio le - - gno è qua - si as - sor - to, il mio
131
le - - gno è qua - si as - sor - - to, men - tre in or - - - ri - da tem -
134
tr
pe - sta il mio le - - - gno e qua - si as - sor - - - - -
137
tr

140
to, giun - ge in por - - to, e 'l li - do af - fer - - - ra, giun - ge in
143
por - to e 'l li - do af - fer - - - - - ra.
148
tr
152
155
D.S.
al Fine

Esser madre è un inferno

L'ARLESIANA

Francesco Cilea
(1866-1950)

18
o - ra, con la fron-te di - mes-sa al pa-vi-men - to,
stentato
e con le pal-me a - per - te, in te con -
f
p
22
rit.
a tempo
con voce soffocata
ver - se, in-vo-can-do il tuo no - me!
Io da quei gior-ni non eb - bi re-quie
p dolce
rit. col canto
mf
27
più.
Sostenuto
con tutta l'anima
Sa - i che gli ho da - to a bra-ni a bra - ni
31
cresc.
poco rit.
a tempo
l'a - ni-ma per far-ne un uom che fos - se o-ne-sto e for - te, a-mo-re e or-go - glio mi - o.
f

Poco più mosso
35
più sentito
I - o t'ho pre - ga-to tan - to, ma sem-pre in va - no! Sa - - i che, se
Poco più mosso
mf
cresc.
più sentito
39
f
muor, né u-n'o-ra gli so-prav-vi - vo, e mo-ri-rò dan-na - ta, e mo-ri-rò dan -
p
f
42
f e più animato
na - ta! Si - - gnor! tu che hai vo - lu - to
[p]
cresc. molto
f e più animato
45 più f
rall. e dim.
p
va - ne le pre-ci mi - e in-si-no ad o - ra e ve - -
f
rall. e dim.

Lento (♩ = 54)
fraseggiando
48
der - mi pian - gen - te e do - lo - ro - sa, ram - men - ta -
Lento (♩ = 54)
p
marcato il canto
f
53
con commozione
-ti, Si - gnor, la ma - dre tua, a - i pie - di del - la cro - ce pro - ster -
f
58
p
implorando con voce soffocata
na - ta!... An - ch'io, Si - gnor, son ma - dre de - so - la - ta. Per pie - tà, ve - glia sul - la vi - ta
f
p
f
p
62
rit.
su - a, per pie - tà, Si - gnor! Si - gnor!
mf
p rit. e dim.
pp

Re dell'abisso, affrettati

UN BALLO IN MASCHERA

Giuseppe Verdi

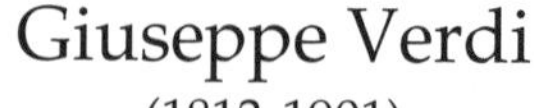

(1813-1901)

Andante sostenuto (♩ = 63)

Ulrica

Re dell'abisso, affrettati, precipita per l'etra, senza libar la

12
fol - - go-re il tet - - - - to mi - - - o pe-ne - -
14
pp
tra.
O-mai tre vol - - te
pp
16
l'u - - pu-pa dal-l'al - - - to so - - spi -
18
rò;
la sa-la-man - - dra i-
pp

20
gni - - vo - ra tre vol - - - - te si - bi -
3
6
22
lò, e del - - - le tom - - - be il
24
ge - mi - to tre vol - - - - te a me par -
f
pp
26
lò! e del - le tom - - - - be il
pp

28
ff
ge - - - mi - to tre vol - - - te a me par -
ff
30
pp
lò, tre vol - te a me, a me par - lò! È
pp
ff
Andante (♩ = 100)
34
declamando
lui! È lui! Ne' pal - pi - ti co - - me ri - sen - to a - des - so
Andante (♩ = 100)
pp
38
la vo - lut - tà ri - ar - de - re del suo tre - men - do am - ples - so!

42
La fa - ce del fu - tu - - - ro nel - la si - ni - stra e -
45
gli ha. M'ar - ri - se al mio scon - giu - ro,
48
ri - fol - go - rar la fa:
sotto voce
nul - la, più
51
nul - la, più nul - la a - scon - der - si al guar - do mi - o po -

54
trà,
nul
la
a
56
ff
scon
der-si
po-trà,
ancora ppp
nul
la, più nul
la,
più
nul-la a-
ff
12
ppp
pp
59
p
scon-der-si
po
trà,
nul
p
61
la
a
fff
scon
ff
6
12

63
ppp
- der - si po - trà,
nul - la a - scon - der - si
ppp
67
f
pp
al guar - do mio po - trà!
Si -
ff
f
71
len - - - zio!
Si - len -
pp
75
- - - zio!
pp
f

Una voce poco fa
IL BARBIERE DI SIVIGLIA

Gioachino Rossini
(1792-1868)

Per le varianti di quest'aria, vedi RICCI: VARIAZIONI, CADENZE, TRADIZIONI (Ricordi).
For the variants of this aria, see RICCI: VARIAZIONI, CADENZE, TRADIZIONI (Ricordi).

17
nò; il mio cor fe-ri-to è già, e Lin-dor fu che il pia-gò. Sì, Lin-
f
22
do - ro mio sa - rà, lo giu - ra - i, la vin - ce -
mf
sf
pp
25
rò; sì, Lin-do - ro mio sa - rà, lo giu -
sf
pp
28
ra - i, la vin - ce - rò. Il tu - tor ri - cu - se -
f
sotto voce
pp
pp

31
rà, io l'in-ge - gno a-guz - ze - rò, al - la fin s'ac - che - te -
33
rà e con-ten - ta io re - ste - rò. Sì, Lin - do - ro mio sa -
sf
36
rà, lo giu - ra - i, la vin - ce - rò; sì, Lin -
pp
39
do - ro mio sa - rà, lo giu - ra - i, la vin - ce - rò.
sf
pp
sf

Moderato
pp dolce
ff
tr
p
pp
f
Io so - no do - ci - le, son ri - spet -
p dolce

58
to - - - sa, so - - - no_ub - bi - dien - - - te,
61
dol - ce, a - mo - ro - - - sa; mi las-scio reg - ge-re, mi la-scio
64
reg - ge-re, mi fo gui-dar, mi_ fo_ gui - dar. Ma se mi
67
f
toc - - ca-no do-v'è il mio de - - bo-le, sa-rò u-na vi - pe - ra,_ sa -
p

70
rò, e cen-to trap - - po-le pri-ma di ce - - de-re fa-rò gio -
73
car, fa - rò gio - car, e cen-to trap - po-le pri-ma di
76
ce - de-re fa-ro gio - car, fa - rò gio - car, e cen-to
79
a piacere
a tempo
trap - po-le pri-ma di ce - de-re, e cen-to trap-po - - le fa - -
col canto
a tempo

82
rò, fa - - rò gio - - - car.
Io so - no
p leggero
85
do - ci-le,
so-no ub-bi - dien-te,
mi la - scio
rinf.
f
88
reg - ge-re,
mi fo gui - dar.
Ma se mi toc - ca-no do-v'è il mio
ff
sf
p
92
f
de - bo-le, sa-rò u-na vi - pe - ra, sa - rò,
e cen-to

95
trap - - po - le pri - ma di ce - - de - re fa - rò gio - car, fa - - rò gio -
98
car, e cen - to trap - - po - le pri - ma di ce - - de - re fa - rò gio -
101
car, fa - rò gio - car, e cen - to trap - - po - le pri - ma di
104
a piacere
a tempo
ce - - de - re, e cen - to trap - po - - le fa - - rò, fa - - rò gio - -
col canto
a tempo

107
car, e cen-to trap-po-le fa-rò gio-car, e cen-to
f
sf
sf
sf
sf
sf
110
trap-po-le fa-rò gio-car, fa-rò gio-car, fa-rò gio-
sf
sf
ff
113
car, fa-rò gio-car.
[col canto]
116

Se Romeo t'uccise un figlio

I CAPULETI E I MONTECCHI

Vincenzo Bellini
(1801 - 1835)

14
par ne dêi la sor - te; ei ne
16
pian - se, e pian - ge an - co - ra. Deh! ti pla - ca, e un al - tro
19
accel.
cresc.
fi - glio tro - ve - ra - i nel mio si - gnor, al - tro fi - glio
f accel. pp cresc.
23
a tempo
cresc. e accel.
tro - ve - rai nel mio - si - gnor, al - tro fi - glio
a tempo
f
pp
f accel. pp
cresc.

a tempo
27
tro - ve - ra - i nel mi-o, nel mio, nel mi - o si - gnor.
a tempo
p
pp
Allegro marziale sostenuto
31
p
mf
ff
34
con forza
La tre-men - da ul-tri - ce
p
38
spa - da a bran-dir Ro - me - o s'ap - pre - - - - sta, e qual

41
fol - go - re fu - ne - sta, mil - le mor - ti ap-por - te -
pp accel.
ff
44
rà. Ma v'ac-cu - si al ciel i - ra - to tan - to
a tempo p
47
san - gue in - van ver - sa - to; e su voi ri - ca - da il
mf
50
san - gue che al - la pa - tria co - ste - rà, che al - la
accel.
ff
pp

53
con forza
pa - tria co - ste - rà. La tre-men-da ul-tri - ce
ff
p
57
spa - da a bran-dir Ro-me-o s'ap-pre - sta, e qual
60
fol - go - re fu - ne - sta, mil - le mor - ti ap-por - te -
pp
accel.
ff
63
rà. Ma v'ac-cu - si al ciel i - ra - to tan - to
a tempo p

66
san - gue in - van ver - sa - to; e su voi ri - ca - da il
mf
69
san - gue che al - la pa - tria co - ste - rà, che al - la
ff
pp
72
Più vivo
pa - tria co - ste - rà. Ma v'ac -
Più vivo
ff
f
75
cu - si tan - to san - gue

78
stringendo sempre
con forza
in - van ver - sa - to; ma su vo - i ri -
pp stringendo sempre
82
con forza cresc.
ca - - da il san - gue che al - la pa - - -
ff
f string. e cresc.
86
tria, al - la pa - - - tria co - - - ste - rà;
ff
[a tempo]
string. sempre
pp assai
90
con forza
ma su vo - i ri - ca - - da il san - gue

94
che al - la pa - - - tria, al - la pa - - - tria co - - - ste -
ff
f string. e cresc.
ff
99
rà, sì, co - ste - rà, sì, co - ste - rà, sì, co - ste -
104
rà, sì, co - ste - rà, sì, co - ste - rà.
109

Nacqui all'affano e al pianto... Non più mesta
LA CENERENTOLA

Gioachino Rossini
(1792-1868)

*Variazione e cadenze di Rossini
Variations and cadenzas by Rossini

co - me un ba - le - - - - - - - - no
19
co - me un ba - le - - - - - - no
ff
ra - pi - do la sor - te mi - - - a,
20
ra - pi - do la sor - te mi - - - a, la sor - te mi - a can -
ff
pp
22
giò, co - me un ba - le - - - - no
p
ff

24
ra - - - - - - - pi - do la sor - te
f
rallentando
mi - a, la sor - te mi - a can - giò.
25
mi - a, la sor - te mi - - a can - giò.
Allegro
Allegro
pp
f
p
27
No, no, no, no, ter - ge - te il ci - glio. Per - ché tre -
31
mar, per - ché tre - mar, per - ché?
A que - sto

34
sen, a que-sto sen vo-la - - - - te;
ff
sf
p
37
fi - glia, so-rel - la, a-mi - ca,
rallentando
tut-to, tut-to, tut-to,
ff
rallentando
41
tut - to tro - - va - te in me, tro - -
pp
44
va - te, tro-va-te in me.
ff a tempo
sf
sf

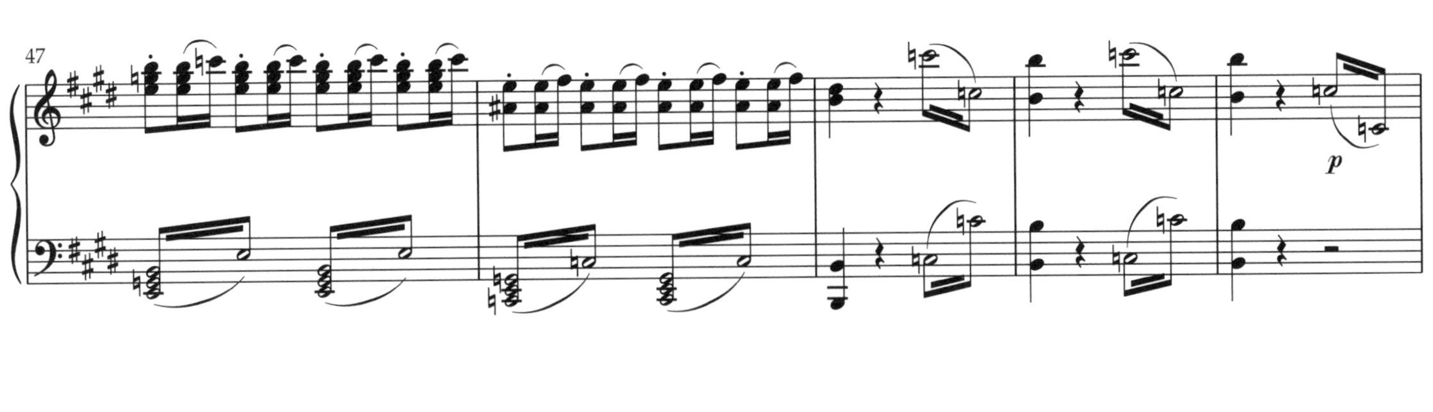
47
p

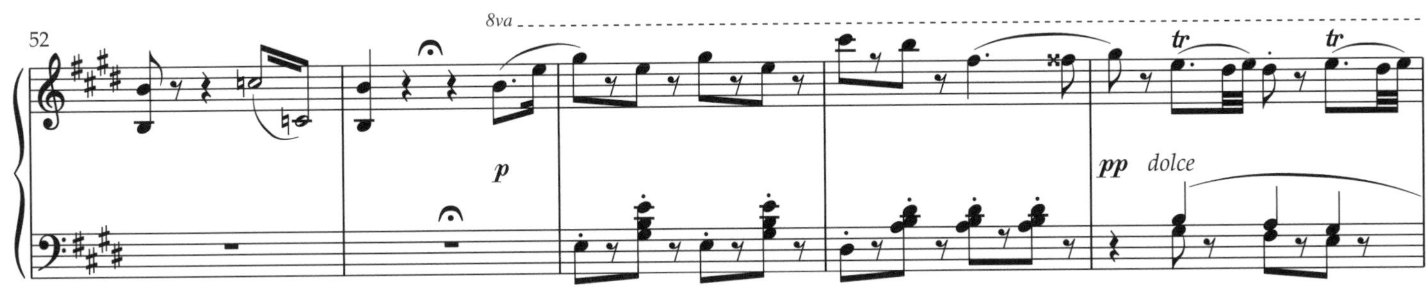
52
8va
p
tr
pp dolce

57
tr
Non più me - sta ac - can - to al fuo - co sta - rò so - la a gor - gheg -
f
p

pp
lam - po, un so - gno, un
61
giar, no. Ah, fu un lam - po, un so - gno, un gio - co il mio lun - go pal - pi -
8va
f
p

65
tar.
Non più me - - sta
ac-can - to al
pp dolce
69
fuo - - co, non più me - sta ac-can - to al fuo - co sta - rò
p
72
so - la a gor - gheg - giar, no. Ah, fu un lam - po, un so - gno, un
8va
f
p
lun - go pal - pi -
75
gio - co il mio lun-go pal-pi -
6
6

77
tar.
Non più me - sta
ac-can - to al
pp dolce
81
fuo - co, non più me - sta ac - can - to al fuo - co sta - rò
pp staccato
84
so - la a gor - gheg - giar.
Ah, fu un lam - po, un so - gno, un
p
lun - go pal - pi - tar.
87
gio - co il mio lun - go pal - pi - tar.
Ah, fu un

90
lam - - - - - po, un so-gno, un gio - - - - -

93
co, ah, fu un lam - po, un so - gno, un gio - co il mio

pal - pi - - - tar, ah, fu un
96
lun - - - - go pal - - - pi - - tar, ah, fu un

99
lam - - - - - - po, un so - gno, un gio - - - - - -
lam - - - - - po, un so-gno, un gio - - - - -
co, ah, fu un lam - po, un so - gno, un
102
co, ah, fu un lam - po, un so - gno, un gio - co il mio
105
lun-go pal - - pi - - tar. Ah, fu un
p

108
gio - co, ah, fu un gio - co, ah, fu un lam - - - - -
ff
111
- - - - - - po il pal-pi - tar, ah, fu un
ff
p
114
gio - co, ah, fu un gio - co, ah, fu un lam - - - - -
ff
117
- - - - - - po il pal-pi - tar, il mi-o
ff
f
f

tar, il lun - go pal - pi -
120
lun - go pal - pi - tar, il mio lun - go pal - pi -
f f ff
tar, il pal - pi - tar, il pal - pi - tar, il pal - pi -
123
tar, il pal - pi - tar, il pal - pi - tar, il pal - pi -
tar.
126
tar.

Torna di Tito a lato

LA CLEMENZA DI TITO

Wolfgang Amadeus Mozart
(1756 - 1791)

18
pro - ve_di_fe - del - tà. Tor - na, tor - na! L'a - cer - bo tuo do -
mf
p
23
lo - re è_ se - gno ma - ni - fe - sto che_ di vir - tù nel
tr
27
co - re l'im - ma - gi - ne ti sta, che_di vir - tù_ nel_ co - re l'im -
p
32
ma - gi - ne ti_ sta. Tor - na, tor - na,___ tor - na_ di_ Ti - to a
tr
tr

37
la - to,
tor - na di Ti - to a
la - to,
tor - na e l'er-ror
pas - sa - to
f
p
42
con re-pli-ca - te e-men - da
pro - ve di fe - del - tà,
46
pro - ve di fe - del - tà,
pro - ve di fe - del - tà.
crescendo
50
Tor - na,
tor - na!
sfp
tr

Parto, ma tu, ben mio

LA CLEMENZA DI TITO

Wolfgang Amadeus Mozart
(1756-1791)

† clarinetto

18
pia - ce,
quel che vor - rai fa - rò,
vor - rai fa -
B
fp
f
21
rò.
p
6
24
Par - to,
ma tu, ben
mi - o,
6
28
me - co
ri - tor - na
in
pa - ce;
sa - rò
qual più
ti
C

32
pia - ce,
quel
che vor - rai
fa - rò, sì,
sa - rò
qual più ti
36
pia - ce,
quel
che vor - rai
fa
rò,
quel
D
40
che
vor - rai fa - rò,
quel
che
vor - rai
fa -
43
rò.
Allegro
E Allegro
f
p

47
fp
50
Guar - da - mi e tut - to o - bli - o, e a ven - di - car - ti io vo - lo, e a
F
f
p
55
tr
tr
ven - di - car - ti io vo - lo;
f
p dolce
G
59
a que - sto sguar - do so - lo da
p

64
me si pen - se - rà, da me si pen - se - rà.
69
Par - to, ma tu ben mi - o, me - co ri - tor - na in
H
fp
74
pa - ce; sa - rò qual più ti pia - ce,
78
quel che vor - rai fa - rò, quel che vor -

82
rai fa - rò. Guar-da-mi, guar-da-mi!
I
J
f
f
p
dolce
87
A que - sto sguar - do so - lo
91
da me si pen - se - rà, da me si pen - se -
96
Allegro assai
rà. Guar-da-mi e tut - to o - bli - o,
Allegro assai
f
p
f

101
e a ven - di-car - ti io vo - lo.
K
p
105
Ah, qual po - ter, oh De - i! do - na - ste al - la bel -
108
tà, do - na - ste al - la bel -
111
ta,
3
3

114
al - la bel - tà, do -
tr
f
p
117
na - - - - - - - - - - - ste al -
120
la bel - tà, do - na - - - ste al -
123
la bel - tà,

126
al - la bel -
f
129
tà. Ah, qual po - ter, oh
M
p
132
Dei! do - na - - - ste al - la bel -
135
tà, do - - - na - - - - - - - ste al -
N
sfp

139
la
bel - - - - - tà,
al - -
142
la
bel - - tà,
al - - la
bel - -
145
tà,
al - - la
bel - - tà.
148

Parto, ma tu ben mio

LA CLEMENZA DI TITO

Wolfgang Amadeus Mozart
(1756-1791)

CLARINETTO IN SI♭

9
H
7
I
f
f
J
p
p
Allegro assai
4
8
K
p
4
L
M
p
N
O
6

Deh, per questo istante solo

LA CLEMENZA DI TITO

Wolfgang Amadeus Mozart
(1756-1791)

15
sde-gno, il tuo ri - gor. Di pie - ta-de in - de - gno è
mf
p
18
ve-ro, sol spi-rar io deg-gio or-ror, sol spi-rar io deg - gio or-ror. Pur sa-re - sti men se -
f
p
cresc.
f
p
21
ve - ro se ve-des - si que-sto cor. Pur sa-re - sti men se - ve - ro, se ve - des - si que-sto
24
cor, se ve-des - si que-sto cor, se ve - des - si
f

27
que - sto cor. Deh, per que - sto i-stan - te so - lo ti ri - cor - da il
31
pri - mo a-mor ché mo - rir mi fa di
34
duo - lo il tuo sde-gno, il tuo ri - gor, il tuo
37
sde-gno, il tuo ri - gor.
Allegro
Allegro
p
mf
f
cresc.

40
Di - - - spe - ra - to va - do a
43
mor - te; ma il mo - rir non mi spa - ven - ta. Il pen -
47
sie - ro mi tor - men - ta che fui te - co un tra - di -
50
tor, che fui te - co un tra - - di - tor!
cresc.
dolce
cresc.

54
(Tan - to af -
58
fan - no sof - fre un co - re, né si mo - re di do - lor!
p
63
Tan - to af - fan - no sof - fre un co - re, né si mo - re di do -
67
lor, di do - lor!)
sf
crescendo

71
Di pie - ta - de in -
fp
p
74
de - - gno, è ve - ro, sol spi - rar io deg - gio or - ror. Pur sa - re - sti men se -
f
p
p
79
ve - ro se ve - des - si que - sto cor. Pur sa - re - sti
84
men se - ve - ro se ve - des - si que - sto
f

88
cor.
(Tan - to af -
dolce
p
93
fan - no sof - fre un co - re, né si mo - re di do - lor!
p
98
Tan - to af - fan - no sof - fre un co - re, nè si mo - re di do -
102
Più allegro
lor, di do - lor!)
Di - spe -
Più allegro
f
p

107
ra - to __ va - do a __ mor - te;
ma il mo -
f
p
111
rir __ non __ mi __ spa - ven - ta.
Il ______ pen - sie - ro
pp
115
mi ______ tor - men - ta che fui te - co un __ tra - di - tor! ____
crescendo
f
p
120
____ (Tan - to af - fan - no sof - fre un co - re, né si __ mo - re __ di __ do - lor,
p

125
né si mo - - re di do - lor, né si
130
mo - - re di do - lor, di do - lor,
f p
p
f
135
di do - lor!)
139

Smanie implacabili

COSÌ FAN TUTTE

Wolfgang Amadeus Mozart
(1756-1791)

Recitativo
Dorabella †
Ah, sco-sta-ti, pa-ven-ta il tri-sto ef-fet-to d'un di-spe-ra-to af - fet - to!
Recitativo
Allegro assai
mf
p
f
tr
4
Chiu-di quel-le fi-ne-stre...
o - dio la lu - ce...
7
o-dio l'a - ria che spi - ro...
o - dio me stes - sa...
10
Chi scher-ni - sce il mio duol...
chi mi con-

† appoggiatura

15
†
Maestoso
so - la?
Deh fug - gi, per pie - tà,
fug - gi,
Maestoso
f
19
fug - gi,
fug - gi per pie - tà,
la - scia - mi so - la.
24
Allegro agitato
Sma - nie im - pla - ca - bi - li
Allegro agitato
6
6
p
27
che m'a - gi - ta - te,
den - tro que -

30
st'a - - ni - ma
più non ces - sa - - te
33
fin - ché l'an - go - - - scia
mi fa mo -
36
rir,
mi fa
mo - rir.
f
39
E - sem - - pio
p
f
p
f
p

42
mi - se - ro
d'a -
f
p
45
mor fu - ne - sto, d'a - mor fu -
48
ne - - sto da - rò al - l'Eu - me - ni - di,
mf
51
se vi - va re - - sto, col suo - no or -

54
ri - - - - - - - bi - le de'
mf
p
57
miei so - - spir, de' miei so - -
60
spir, de' miei so - - spir!
crescendo
63
Sma - nie im - pla -
f
p

66
ca - - bi - li
che m'a - gi - ta - - - te,
69
en - - tro que - st'a - - ni - ma
più non ces -
72
sa - - te
fin - ché l'an - go - - - scia
mfp
mfp
75
mi fa mo - rir,
mi fa
mo -

78
rir.
E -
f
p
81
sem - - - pio mi - - se - ro
84
d'a - mor fu - ne - - sto, d'a -
87
mor fu - ne - - sto da - rò al - l'Eu -

90
me - - ni - di,
se vi - va re - - - sto,
mf
p
mfp
mf
p
93
col suo - no or - ri - - - - - - - - bi -
mfp
crescendo
96
le de' miei so - - - spir, da - rò al - l'Eu -
f
p
crescendo
99
me - - ni - di,
se vi - va re - - - sto,
f

102
col suo - no or - ri - bi - le
p
105
de' miei so - spir, da - rò al - l'Eu - me - ni - di,
crescendo
108
se vi - va re - - sto,
f
111
col suo - no or - ri - - bi - le, col
p
sf
p

114
suo - - no or - - ri - - - - bi - le de'
117
miei so - - spir, de'
6
120
miei so - - spir, de' miei so -
123
spir.

O don fatale
DON CARLO

Giuseppe Verdi
(1813-1901)

12
Più mosso (♩ = 126)
tà! Ver-sar, ver - sar sol pos - so il pian - to, spe-me non
té! Tom-bez, tom - bez, lar - mes a - mè - res! Mes tra-hi -
Più mosso (♩ = 126)
p
15
ho, sof - frir do - vrò! Il mio de-lit - to è or-ri - bil
sons et mes for-faits, mes souil-lu - res et mes mi -
18
tan - to che can - cel - lar mai nol po - trò! Ti ma-le -
sè - res, vous ne les la-ve - rez ja-mais, ja - mais! Je te mau -
f
21
di - co, ti ma-le-di - co, o mia bel-tà, ah, ti ma-le -
dis, je te mau-dis, je te mau-dis, ah! je te mau -
f

24
[𝄐]
di - co, o mia bel - tà!
dis, ô ma beau - té!
3
p
28
Molto meno mosso (𝅗𝅥 = 84)
cantabile
O mia Re - gi - na, io t'im - mo -
A - dieu, Rei - ne, vic - ti - me
Molto meno mosso (𝅗𝅥 = 84)
p
pp
34
f
3
pp
3
la - i al fol - le er - ror di que - sto cor. So - lo in un
pu - re de mes dé - loy - a - les et fol - les a - mours! Dans un cou -
f
pp
40
f
3
p
chio - stro al mon - do o - ma - i do - vrò ce - lar il mi - o do -
vent et sous la bu - re, je m'en - se - ve - lis pour tou - jours, pour tou -
f
pp

46
pp
lor! Ohi - mè! Ohi - mè! O mia Re - gi - na, so - lo in un
jours! A - dieu, a - dieu. Reine, a - dieu! dans un cou -
ppp
52
cresc.
chio - stro al mon - do o - ma - i do - vrò ce - lar il mi - o do -
vent et sous la bu - re, dans un cou - vent et sous la
p poco string.
58
lo - re! Ah! so - lo in un chio - stro al mon - do o - ma - i do - vrò ce -
bu - re! Ah! je m'en se - ve - lis pour tou-jours, pour tou - jours! dans un cou -
62
Allegro più mosso (𝅗𝅥 = 152)
lar il mi - o do - lor!
vent pour tou-jours, pour tou - jours!
Allegro più mosso (𝅗𝅥 = 152)
mf

65
Oh ciel! E Car-lo? a
Et Car-los?
pp
69
mor-te do-ma-ni... gran Dio! a mor-te an-dar ve-
Oui! de-main, peut-ê-tre, il tom-be-ra sous le fer sa-
72
drò! Ah! Un dì mi re-sta, la
cre! Ah! Un jour me res-te! Oui!
crescendo
col canto
ff
76
lunga
con slancio
ff
spe-me m'ar-ri-de! Si-a be-ne-
je me sens re-naî-tre! Ah! je me
8va
f
ff

79
det - - - - to il ciel, be-ne-det - to il ciel! Lo sal - ve -
sens re - naî - tre! bé-ni ce jour je le sau - ve -
(8)
82
rò! Un dì mi re-sta, un dì mi re-sta, ah, si -
rai! Un jour me res-te, un jour me res-te, bé-ni ce
mf
f
f
85
a be-ne-det - to il ciel! Lo sal - ve-rò!
jour, bé - ni ce jour, je le sau - ve-rai!
ff
90

Mura felici
LA DONNA DEL LAGO

Gioachino Rossini
(1792-1868)

13
ben s'ag - gi - ra!
Do - po più lu - ne io vi ri - veg - go.
16
Ah! vo - i più al guar - do mio non
19
sie - te co - me lo fo - ste un dì, ri - den - ti, e lie - te!
22
Qui nac - que, fra voi creb - be, l'in - no - cen - te mio ar - dor.

25
Quan-to so - a - ve fra voi scor-rea mia
p
ff
28
vi - ta al fian-co di co - le - i, che ri-spon-dea pie - to - sa a' vo - ti
mf
31
Allegro
mie - i!
Allegro
p
ff
34
Ne - mi - co nem - bo, or vi rat-tri - sta e ag-ghiac-cia il po - ve - ro mio cor!

37
Ma - no cru - de - le a voi to - glie,
ff
p
40
a me in-vo - la...
oh, rio mar-to - - - - - - - ro!
la
10
mf
f
43
a piacere
vo - stra a - bi - ta - tri - ce,
il mio te - so - ro.
ff
col canto
Andantino
46
ff
tr
p

49

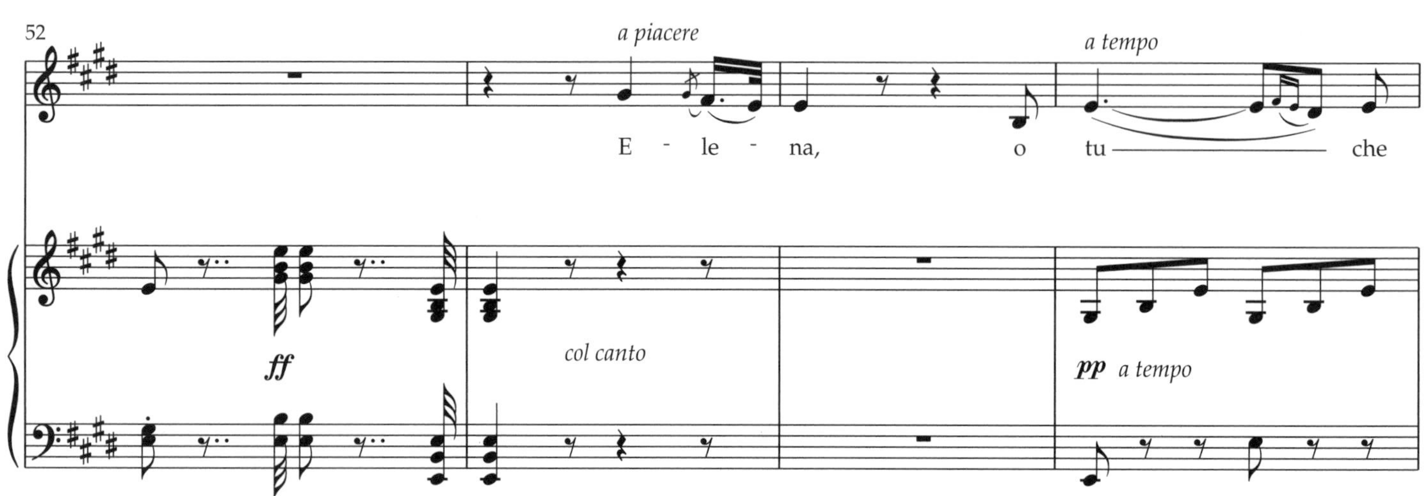
52
a piacere
a tempo
E - le - na, o tu — che
ff
col canto
pp a tempo

56
chia - - mo, o tu — che chia - - mo! Deh, vo - la a

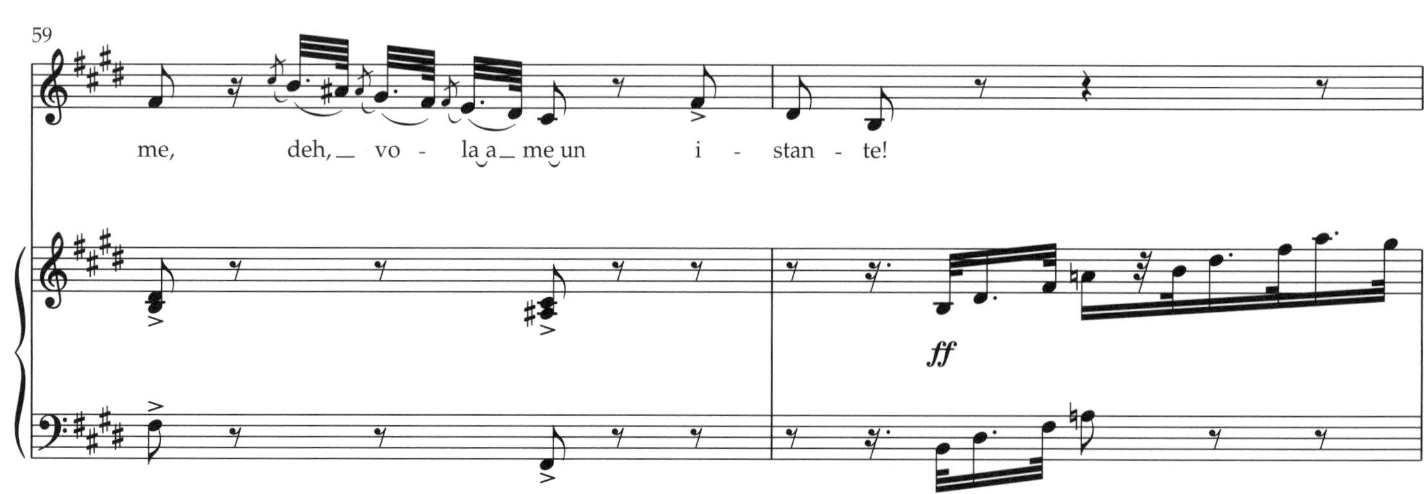
59
me, deh, — vo - la a — me un i - stan - te!
ff

61
p
63
Tor - - na - mi a dir "io t'a - mo."
simile
65
Ser - - - ba - mi la tua fé!
f
E al -
67
lor di te si - cu - - - - - ro,

69
a - - - ni - ma mia, lo giu - - - - - - ro, ti
71
to - - - glie - rò al più for - - - - te, o mo - ri -
f
73
rò, o mo - ri - rò per te, ti
p
simile
75
to - - - glie - rò al più for - te, o mo - ri -

77
rò, o mo - ri - ro per te.
ff
[mf]
79
Gra - - ta a me fi - - - - a, mi
pp sotto voce
82
fia la mor - - - - - te s'E - le - na
p
84
mi - - - - a, s'E - le - na mi - - - - a, s'E - le - na
3
3

86
mi - - - a non è, s'E-le-na mi - - - - a, s'E-le-na
89
mi - - - - a, s'E-le-na mia, no, non è.
ff
f
p
p
92
ff
Allegro
p
96
tr
f
p
simile

99
102
p
Oh, quan - te la - gri-me fi - nor ver - sa - i lun - gi lan -
tr
ff
p
simile
105
guen-do da' tuoi bei ra - i! O-gn'al-tro og - get - to è a me fu -
108
ne - sto, tut-to è im-per - fet - to, tut - to de - te - sto; di lu - ce il

111
cie - - - - - lo, no, più non bril - - - - - - la, più non sfa -
113
tr
vil - - - - - la a - stro per me, no;
p
115
tr
di lu - ce il cie - lo, no, più non
simile
118
bril - la, più non sfa - vil - la a - stro per me,

121
no, no, no, per me.
123
Ca - - - ra! tu so - la mi dai la
126
cal-ma, tu ren - - - di al -
crescendo
129
l'al - ma gra - ta mer-cé! tu
f

132
ren - - di gra - - ta mer - cé! Oh, quan - te
ff
135
tr
la - gri-me fi - nor ver - sa - i lun - gi lan - guen-do da' tuoi bei -
p
simile
138
ra - i! O - gn'al-tro og - get - to è a me fu - ne - sto, tut-to è im-per -
141
fet - to, tut - to de - te - sto; di lu - ce il cie - - - lo, no, più non

144
bril - - - la, più non sfa - vil - - - la a - stro per
tr
146
me, no;
di lu - ce il
p
tr
simile
149
cie - lo no più non bril - la, più non sfa - vil - la a - stro per
152
me, no, no, no, per

154
me!
Ca - ra! tu
so - la
mi dai la
cal - ma,
tu ren-di al -
p
cresc.
ff
157
l'al - ma
gra - ta mer - cé!
p
159
crescendo
161
sì!
tu
ren - di al - l'al - - - - ma
gra - ta mer -
ff

163
cé.
Ca - ra! tu so - la mi dai la cal - ma, tu ren-di al -
p
cresc.
ff
166
l'al - ma gra - ta mer - cé!
p
168
170
sì, tu ren - di al - l'al - ma gra - ta mer -
ff

172
cé, gra - - - - ta mer - - - -
f
f
f
f
174
cé, gra - - - - ta mer - - - -
f
f
f
f
176
cé, gra - ta mer - - cé, gra - ta mer -
ff
178
cé, gra - ta mer - cé!

Tanti affetti in tal momento

LA DONNA DEL LAGO

Gioachino Rossini
(1792-1868)

11
pos - so, io non pos - so a te spie - - gar.
Deh! il si-
6
13
len - - zio sia lo-qua - - - - ce... tut - to
15
di - ca un tron - co ac - cen - - - - to... Ah, si-
17
gnor! la bel - - la pa - ce tu sa-

19
pe - sti a me do - nar, tu sa -
21
pe - sti a me do-nar, tu sa - - - -
f
23
pe - sti a me do-nar, a me do -
tr
25
nar, a me do - nar, tu sa -
tr
cresc.
ff

27
a piacere
pe - - - - - - - - - sti a me
sf
ff col canto
29
Allegro
do - nar!
Allegro
p sotto voce
31
ff
ff
34
ff

37
Fra il pa - - dre e fra l'a -
p
40
man - te, oh, qual be - a - - to i stan - - - - - -
ff
43
- - - - - - - te!
p
46
Ah! chi spe - rar po - te - - - - a, ah! chi spe - rar po -
simile

49
te - - - a
tan - ta
fe - li - ci - tà,
52
tan - ta
fe - li - ci - ta!
ff
p sotto voce
simile
55
ff
58
f

61
Fra il pa - - - dre, e fra l'a man - - - - te, oh,
p
64
qual be - - - a - - - to i - - - stan - - - - - - - -
ff
66
- - - - - - - - - - - - te!
68
Ah! chi spe - rar po - te - - - - a,
p
simile

71
ah! chi spe-rar po-te - - - a tan-ta fe-li-ci-
74
a piacere
tà, tan-ta fe-li-ci-tà!
a tempo
col canto
a tempo
p sotto voce
simile
77
ff
ff
81
f
84
Fra il pa - - - dre e fra l'a - man - - - te oh qual be -
p sotto voce
simile
87
a - - - - - - to i - - - - stan - - - - - - -
a piacere
ff col canto

89
te!
91
Ah! chi spe - rar po - te - - - - a,
p a tempo
simile
94
ah chi spe - rar po - te - - - - a,
tan - ta fe - li - ci -
97
a piacere
tà,
col canto

98
a tempo
tan - ta fe - li - ci - tà! Fra il pa - dre, e fra l'a -
a tempo
p sotto voce
simile
101
man - te, oh, qual be - a - to i - stan - te! Ah!
104
chi spe - rar po - te - a tan - ta fe - li - ci -
107
tà! Fra il pa - dre, e fra l'a - man - te oh

110
qual be - a - to i - stan - te! Ah chi spe - rar po -
113
te - a tan - - - ta fe - li - ci - tà! Ah!
ff
116
chi spe - rar po - tea tan - - -
118
tr
ta fe - li - ci - tà! Ah!

120
tr
tr
tr
tr
chi spe - - rar po - - tea tan - - -
122
3
3
ta fe - li - ci - tà, fe - - - -
f
f
124
li - - - - ci - - - - tà, fe - - -
f
f
ff
126
li - - - ci - - - - tà, fe - li - ci -

128
[ten.]
tà, fe - - li - - ci - - tà, fe - - - li - - ci -
[col canto]
130
tà!
[a tempo]
132
134
3
3
3
3
136

Tu il cuor mi strazi

EDGAR

Giacomo Puccini
(1858-1924)

19
be - la - - - va al - l'av - - - vol - to - - - -
a tempo
pp
23
io nel - l'a - go - nia l'a - gnel...
tr
cresc. molto
27
ff con slancio
32
A - - gnel - lin, fa - i pie - tà, fai pie - tà!
pp
f

37
stent. molto
Più allegro
Ah! Ah! Ah!
Più allegro
stent. molto
tr
f
ff
p
pp
43
49
Andante mosso
rit.
a tempo
Sia per voi l'o - ra - zion, è per me
Andante mosso
pp
55
la can - zon! Vo' can - tar, vo' tril - lar!

61
a tempo
rit.
a tempo
Vo' can - tar, vo' tril - lar! Chi non vuo - le a - scol -
pp
66
tar tor - ni in chie - sa a pre - gar! Chi non vuo - le a - scol - tar tor - ni in
pp
71
chie - sa a pre - gar!
76
Sostenendo
L'i - ra vo - - - - stra o il per - don
Sostenendo
f a tempo
m.d.
m.s.
6
6
6

80
io del par sprez - ze - rò! L'ab - bor -
m.s.
85
ri - ta can - zon, ah! can - te -
m.s.
m.s.
91
rallentando
rò. Vo' can - tar, vo' tril - lar! Vo' can - tar, vo' tril - lar! chi non
8va
rallentando
p
legato
96
vuo - le a - scol - tar tor - ni in chie - sa a pre - gar!
rit. e dim.

O mio Fernando

LA FAVORITA

Gaetano Donizetti
(1797-1848)

16
Sì!
Lui...
Tut - to mel
Tout me l'at -
f
p
Lento
21
di - ce, e dub-bia è l'al-ma an-co - ra al - l'i-nat - te - sa gio-ia! Oh
teste et mon coeur doute en - co - re de ce bon-heur i-nat-ten-du.
Lento
p
25
Moi, l'é - pou - ser! Ah! ce se - rait in - fâ - me! Moi, lui por - ter en
Di - o! Spo-sar - lo? Oh, mia ver - go-gna e stre - ma! In do - te al
p
29
dot mon dés-hon - neur! Non, non; dût - il me fuir a - vec hor -
Allegro
pro - de re-car il di - so - nor— no, ma - i; do - ves - se e - se -
Allegro
f

32
reur, il con-naî-tra la mal-heu-reu-se fem-me qu'il croit di-gne de son cœur.
crar-mi, fug-gir, sa-prà in bre-v'o-ra chi sia la don-na che co-tan-to a-do-ra.
f

Cantabile

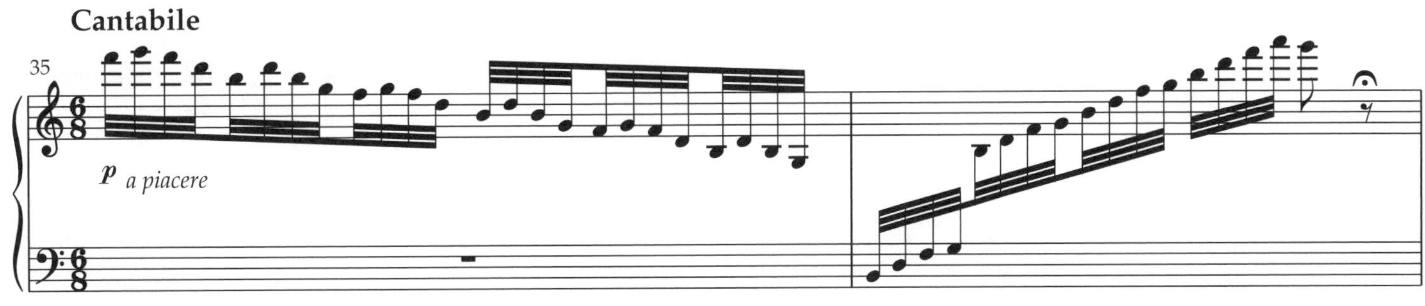
35
p a piacere

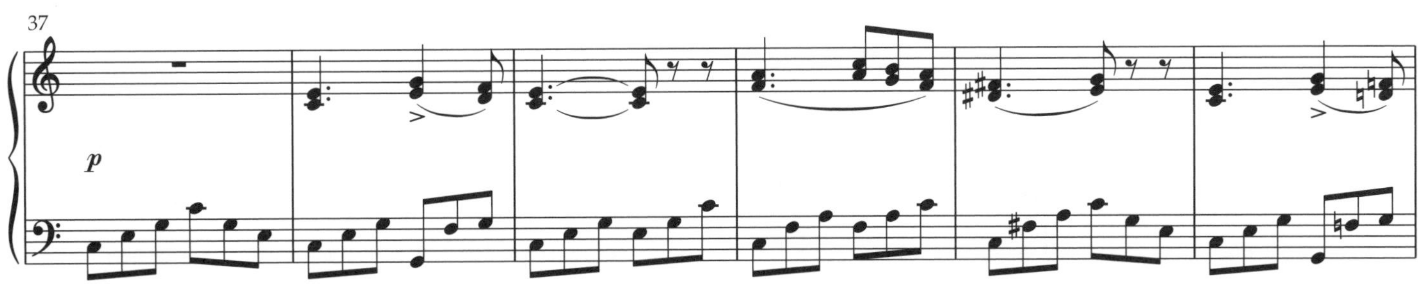
37
p

43
O mio Fer-nan-do!
O mon Fer-nand!

48
Del - la ter - ra il tro - no a pos - se - der - ti a - vri - a do - na - to il
tous les biens de la ter - re, pour être à toi mon cœur eût tout don -
53
cor; ma pu - ro l'a - mor mi - o co - me il per - do - no,
né; mais mon a - mour, plus pur que la pri - è - re,
58
dan - na - to, ahi las - sa! è a di - spe - ra - to or - ror.
au dé - ses - poir, hé - las! hé - las! est con - dam - né.
p
62
Il ver fia no - to, e in tuo di - spre - gio e -
Tu sau - ras tout, et par toi mé - pri -

65
stre - mo la pe - na a - vrom - mi
sé - e, j'au-rai souf - fert tout,
68
rall.
[a piacere]
a tempo
che mag - gior si de', ah!
Se il giu - sto tuo di -
tout ce qu'on peut souf - frir. Ah!
Si ta jus -
rall.
[col canto]
p a tempo
72
sde - gno al - lor, al - lor fia sce - mo, ah!
ti - ce est a - lors a - pai - sé - e, mon
75
rall.
piom - bi, gran Di - o, piom - bi, gran Di - o, la fol - gor tua su
Dieu! fais - moi mou - rir, mon Dieu! mon Dieu! fais - moi, fais-moi mou -
col canto

78
a tempo
me, ah! se fia sce - mo il tuo di - sde - gno, piom - bi, o Dio, la fol - gor tua su
rir, si ta jus - tice est a - pai - sé - e, mon Dieu! mon Dieu! fais - moi mou -
a tempo
81
me, ah! se fia sce - mo il tuo di - sde - gno, piom - bi, o Di - o, la fol - gor tua su
rir, si ta jus - tice est a - pai - sé - e, mon Dieu! mon Dieu! fais - moi, fais-moi mou -
84
recitativo
me. Su, cru - de - le, e chi v'ar - re - sta? Scrit - to è in
rir. Ve - nez, cru - els! qui vous ar - rê - te? ve -
p
recitativo
f
88
con forza
Moderato mosso
cie - lo il mio do - lor! Scrit - to è in ciel il mio do -
nez, cru - els, ve - nez! Mon ar - rêt descend du
Moderato mosso
p
f

91
lor! Su, ve - ni - - - te, el-l'è u - na fe - sta, spar - sa
ciel. Ve - nez tous, c'est u - ne fê - te! de bou-
p
94
l'a - - - ra sia di fior. Già la tom - - ba a me s'ap-
quets pa - rez l'au - tel. Qu'u - ne tombe aus - si s'ap-
fp
97
pre - sta; ri - co - per - - ta in ne - gro vel sia la
prê - te! Et je - tez un voi - le noir sur la
100
tri - - sta fi - dan - za - ta che re - iet - ta, di - spe-
tris - - te fi - an - cé - e qui mau - dite et re - pous-
f
fp

103
p
ra - ta, non a - vrà per - do - no in ciel, ma - le-det -
sé - e, se - ra mor - te a - vant ce soir, qui mau-di -
p
106
ta, di - spe-ra - ta, non a - vrà per-do - no in ciel, no, non a -
te, re - pous-sé - e, se - ra morte a-vant ce soir, a - vant ce
109
accel. e cresc.
vrà, ma - le-det - ta, di - spe-ra - ta, non a - vrà per-do - no in
soir, qui mau-di - te, re - pous-sé - e, se - ra morte a-vant ce
accel. e cresc.
112
ff
ciel, non a - vrà per-do - no in ciel ah! non a - vrà per - do - no in
soir, se - ra morte a-vant ce soir, ah! se - ra morte a - vant ce
f
p

115
Allegro
ciel.
soir.
Allegro
f
119
Ah! cru - de - li, e chi v'ar - re - sta?
Pour ban - deau de fi - an - cé - e,
123
Scrit - to in cie - lo è il mio do - lor,
qu'on me jette un voi - le noir,
127
scrit - to in cie - lo è il mio do - lor!
qu'on me jette un voi - le noir.

131
Cru -
135
de - li, ve - ni - te.
Ve - nez cru - els
Scrit - to è in
Mon ar -
Moderato mosso
140
ciel il mio do - lor. Su, ve - ni - te, el - lè u - na
rêt des - cend du ciel. Ve - nez tous, c'est u - ne
Moderato mosso
143
fe - sta, spar - sa l'a - ra sia di fior. Già la
fê - te! de bou - quets pa - rez l'au - tel. Qu'u - ne

146
tom - - - ba a me s'ap - pre - sta; ri - co - per - ta in ne - gro
tombe aus - si s'ap - prê - te! Et je - tez un voi - le
149
vel sia la tri - sta fi - dan - za - ta, che re -
noir sur la tris - te fi - an - cé - e qui, mau -
f
152
iet - ta, di - spe - ra - ta, non a - vrà per - do - no in
dite et re - pous - sé - e, se - ra mor - te a - vant ce
p
fp
155
ciel, ma - le - det - ta, di - spe - ra - ta, non a - vrà per - do - no in
soir, qui mau - di - te, re - pous - sé - e, se - ra morte a - vant ce

158
ciel, no, non a - vrà, ma - le-det - ta, di - spe-ra -
soir, a - vant ce soir, qui mau-di - te, re - pous-sé -
161
accel. e cresc.
ff
ta, non a - vrà per-do - no in ciel, non a - vrà per-do - no in ciel, ah! non a -
e, se - ra morte a-vant ce soir, se - ra morte a-vant ce soir, ah! se - ra
accel. e cresc.
164
Più mosso
vrà per-do - no in ciel. Ah! la tri - sta fi - dan -
morte a - vant ce soir. Ve - nez, cru -
Più mosso
p
f
167
za - ta non a - vrà, non a - vrà per - do - no in
els, ve - nez! Qu'on me jette un voi - le

170
ciel, ah! non a - vrà per-do - no in ciel, ah! non a - vrà per - do - no in
noir, cru - els ve - nez, ve - nez! cru-els ve - nez, ve -
174
ciel, ma - le-det - ta di - spe - ra -
nez! la fi - an - cé -
oppure
ta non a - vrà per - do - no in ciel.
e se - ra morte a - vant ce soir.
177
ta, non a - vrà per - do - no in ciel.
e se - ra morte a - vant ce soir.
181

Al suon del tamburo

LA FORZA DEL DESTINO

Giuseppi Verdi
(1813-1901)

23
bel - la la guer - ra! Ev - vi - va la guer - ra, ev - vi - - - -
28
va!
34
lunga
lunga
È so - lo o - bli - a - to da
pp
40
vi - le chi muo - re; al bra - vo sol - da - to, al ve - ro va - lor è

46
3
premio serbato di gloria, d'onor! È bella la
51
f
guerra, evviva la guerra, evviva la guerra, evvi-
56
va!
f
62
lunga
Se vieni, fra-
lunga
sf
p

68
tel - lo, sa - rai ca - po - ra - le; e tu co - lon - nel - lo, e tu ge - ne - ra - le. Il
pp
75
leggerissimo
di - o fur - fan - tel - lo dal - l'ar - co im - mor - ta - le fa - rà di cap - pel - lo al
81
bra - vo uf - fi - zial! È bel - la la guer - ra, è bel - la la
p
86
f
guer - ra! Ev - vi - va la guer - ra, ev - vi - - - - - va!
f
sf

Presti omai
GIULIO CESARE

George Frideric Handel
(1685-1759)

a cura di J.M.B.

13
tor, le sue pal - - - - - - - - - - - -
15
- - - - - - - - - - - - me, le sue
17
pal - me, le sue pal - - me al vin - - ci - tor!
f
20
Pre - sti o - ma - i l'E - gi - zia ter - ra le sue pal - me,
p

23
le sue pal - - - - - - - - - - me,
f
26
le sue pal - me al vin - ci - tor, le sue pal - - - - -
p
28
30
- - me, le sue pal - - me al vin - - ci - tor! Pre - sti o - mai
f
p

33
l'E - gi - zia ter - - - - ra le sue pal - - - - - - -
36
- - - - - - - - - - - - - -
39
- - - - - - me, pres - ti o - mai l'E - gi - zia ter - ra le sue
42
pal - me al vin - ci - tor, le sue

44
pal - me,
le sue pal - me al vin - ci - tor,
f
p
46
le sue pal - me al vin - ci - tor!
f
49
52

Il padre adorato
IDOMENEO

Wolfgang Amadeus Mozart
(1756-1791)

13

ror, ___ fre - men - do,

fp *cresc.* *f* *p*

16

fre - men - - do d'or - ror.

crescendo *f* *p*

19

Mo - ri - re cre - de - i di ___

simile

22

gio - ia e d'a - mo - re, di gio - ia e d'a -

25
mo - re: or, bar - - - ba - - ri
p
crescendo
27
De - i! m'uc -
f
p
sfp
sfp
30
ci - - de il do - lor, m'uc -
sfp
sfp
33
ci - - de il do - lor, m'uc - ci - de il do - lor, m'uc -

37
ci - - de il do - lor.
42
Il pa - - - - dre a - do -
44
ra - to ri - tro - vo, e lo
f
p
47
per - do, e lo per - do. Mi
f
p
tr
fp

51
fug - - ge, sde - gna - to, fre - men - - do d'or -
tr
fp
54
ror, fre - men - do,
cresc.
f
p
57
fre - men - - do d'or - ror.
crescendo
60
Mo - ri - re cre - de - i di
simile

63
gio - ia e d'a - mo - re, mo - ri - re cre -
sfp
66
de - i di gio - - - ia, di gio - - - ia e d'a -
sfp
p
69
mo - re: or, bar - - - ba - - - ri
crescendo
71
De - i! m'uc -
f
p
sfp
sfp

74
ci - - de il do - lor,
m'uc -
sfp
sfp
77
ci - - de il do - lor,
m'uc - ci - - de il do - lor,
m'uc -
81
ci - de il do - lor,
m'uc - ci - de il do - lor,
m'uc - ci - de il do -
86
lor.
mf
mfp
mf
mfp
pp

A dio, Roma

L'INCORONAZIONE DI POPPEA

Claudio Monteverdi
(1567-1643)

a cura di P.T.

16
ra - ta, di-spe-ra - ta i sor - di ma - ri.
[Moderato]
19
L'a - ria, che d'o-ra in o - ra ri-ce-ve-rà i miei fia - ti, li por-te-rà, per
[Moderato]
[mf]
22
no - me del cor mi - o, a ve - der, a ba-ciar le pa - trie mu - ra.
25
Lentamente
Ed i - o sta - rò so - lin - ga al - ter - nan - do le mos - se ai
Lentamente
[p]

29
pian - ti, ai pas - si, in - se - gnan - do pie - ta - de ai tron - chi e ai sas - si.
Recitativo
33
Re - mi - ga - te, re - mi - ga - te, re - mi - ga - te og - gi mai, per - ver - se gen - ti! Al - lon - ta - na - te - vi,
Recitativo
[mf]
[cresc.]
[f]
36
al - lon - ta - na - te - vi o - ma - i da... da... da - gli a - ma - ti li - di.
[dim.]
[mp]
[p]
[Più mosso]
40
Ahi, ahi, ahi, sa - cri - le - go duo - lo, tu, tu, tu m'in - ter - di - ci il
[Più mosso]
[f]

43
pian - to quan - do la - scio la pa - tria, tu m'in - ter - di - ci 'l pian - to quan - do
46
la - scio la pa - tria, né stil - lar u - na la - cri - ma pos - s'i - o,
[dim.]
[mp]
50
men - tre di - co a' pa - ren - ti e a Ro - ma, né stil - lar u - na la - cri - ma pos - s'i - o
[p]
[f]
54
men - tre di - co a' pa - ren - ti e a Ro - ma: a di - o!
[mp]
[p]

Cruda sorte! Amor tiranno!

L'ITALIANA IN ALGERI

Gioachino Rossini
(1792-1868)

13
ri - glio. Da chi spe - ro, oh Dio!_con - si - glio? oh Dio!_con-
16
si - glio? Chi con - for - to mi da -
18
rà? Da chi spe - - ro, oh Dio! con -
ff
p
20
si - glio? Chi con - for - to mi da - -

22
rà? Da chi spe - ro, oh Dio! con -
6
3
24
si - glio? Chi con - for - to mi da - rà?
Allegro
27
ff
p
30
Qua ci vuol di-sin-vol-tu-ra,
f

35
non più sma-nie, né pa - u - ra:
di co-rag-gio è tem-po a - des-so,
39
or chi so - no si ve - drà,
or chi so - no si ve - drà.
43
Già so per pra - ti - ca qual sia l'ef - fet - to d'un sguar-do
p
simile
46
lan - gui - do, d'un so - spi - ret - to... So a do - mar gli uo - mi - ni co - me si

49
fa, sì, sì, sì, sì, so a do-mar gli uo - mi - ni co - me si
52
fa, sì, so a do - mar gli uo-mi-ni co - me si fa.
sf
(p)
p
55
Sien dol - ci o ru - vi-di, sien flem - ma o
58
fo - co, son tut - ti si - mi - li a pres-so a po - co... sien flem-ma o
crescendo
rinf.
f

61
fo - co, son tut - ti si - mi-li a pres-so a po - co... Tut - ti la
sf
sf
64
chie - do-no, tut - ti la bra - ma-no, tut - ti la chie - do-no, tut - ti la
p
67
bra - ma-no da va - ga fem - mi - na fe - li - ci - tà, sì, sì, sì,
70
sì, da va - ga fem - mi - na fe - li - ci -

72
tà, sì, da va - ga fem - mi - na fe - li - ci -
sf
74
tà. Tut - ti la bra - ma - no, tut - ti la chie - do - no da va - ga
p
77
fem - mi - na fe - li - ci - tà, tut - ti la bra - ma - no, tut - ti la
80
chie - do - no da va - ga fem - mi - na fe - li - ci -

82
tà, fe - li - ci - tà, fe - li - ci - tà, da va-ga
ff
85
fem-mi-na fe-li - ci - tà, da va-ga fem-mi-na fe-li - ci -
88
tà, fe - li - ci - tà, fe - li - ci -
90
tà, fe - li - ci - tà.

Cari luoghi ov'io passai

LINDA DI CHAMOUNIX

Gaetano Donizetti
(1797-1848)

22
dì __ che tor - ne - rò. Ad - di - - - o, ad - di - -
27
o! Per sua
p
fz
fz
p
32
ma - dre an - dò u - na fi - glia mi - glior sor - te a rin - trac - ciar. Col - le
36
la - gri - me al - le ci - glia le __ do - len - ti si ab - brac - ciâr. Pen - sa a
calando
p

40
me, di-cea la ma - dre, ser - ba in-tat - to il tuo can-do - re; nei ci-men - ti del - l'a-
simile
45
Maggiore
mo - re vol - gi al Nu - me il tuo pre - gar.
Maggiore
p
p
49
Ei non
52
rall.
puo - te a buo - na fi - glia la sua gra - zia, la sua gra-zia ri-cu -
f
p [col canto]

55
Poco più
sar.
Poco più
f
p
59
I° Tempo - Meno
Que' con - si - gli, ahi, trop - po po - co la fan -
I° Tempo - Meno
p
62
ciul - la ram - men - tò. Nel suo cor s'ac - ce - se un
65
fo - co che la pa - ce le in vo - lò. La tra -
calando

68
di - ta al - lor ri - tor - na, cer - ca in - van di ma - dre un se - no; di ri -
simile
72
rall.
Maggiore
[a tempo]
mor - si il cor ri - pie - no u - na tom - ba, u - na tom - ba ri - tro - vò. Sul - la
Maggiore
rall.
p [a tempo]
76
tom - ba fin - ché vis - se quel - la me - sta la - gri - mò, sul - la
80
rall.
Poco più
tom - ba fin - ché vis - se quel - la me - sta, quel - la me - sta la - gri - mò. Sul - la
Poco più
f
p rall.
pp

84
tom-ba, sul-la tom-ba fin-ché vis-se,
ah!
p
88
quel - la me-sta la - gri -
f
ff
91
mò, la - gri-mò, la - gri - mò, quel-la me-sta la-gri - mò, la - gri-mò, la - gri -
f
94
mò, me-sta la - gri - mò.
ff

Giusto ciel, in tal periglio

MAOMETTO II

Gioachino Rossini
(1792-1868)

17
f
rar la tu - a pie - - tà, im - plo -
f
20
f
rar la tu - a pie - tà;
f
23
più con -
26
si - glio, più spe - ran - za non m'a - van - za che pian -

29
gen - do, che ge - men - do im - plo - rar la
32
tu - a pie - ta, im - plo - rar la
35
tu - a pie - tà, im - plo - rar la
38
tu - a pie - tà.
pp sotto voce

Addio, o miei sospiri

ORFEO ED EURIDICE

Christoph Willibald von Gluck
(1714-1787)

15
spi - ri, han spe - me i miei de - si - ri; per
19
lei sof - frir vo' tut - to, ed o - - - gni
p
22
duo - - lo sfi - dar! Ad - dio, ad - dio, o miei so -
mf
dolce
25
spi - ri, han spe-me i miei de - si - ri; per

28
lei vo' tut - to o - sa - - - - - - - - -
31
- - - - - - - - - - - - - - -
34
- - - - - - - - - re, ed o - gni duo - lo e pe -
37
ri - glio sfi - dar! Io vo da l'a - tre spon - de var -
mf

41
car di Sti - ge l'on - de,
e
f
45
de_ l'or - ren - do Tar-ta-ro le Fu - rie_ su - pe - rar!
Per
p
f
49
lei vo' tut - to o - sa - - - - - - - - -
52
- - - - - - - - - - - re e tut - ti

55
tr
vo' sfi - dar!
58
61
Ad - dio, ad - dio, o miei so -
p
65
spi - ri, han spe - me i miei de - si - ri; per

69
lei sof - frir vo' tut - to, ed o - gni duol sfi - dar, ed
f
p
73
o - - - - - - - - - - - - gni
76
duol sfi - dar! Ad - dio, ad - dio, o miei so -
f
p
79
spi - ri, han spe-me i miei de - si - ri; per
f p
f p

82
lei vo' tut - to o - sa
86
89
- re, ed o - gni duo - lo sfi - dar! Io vo da l'a - tre
cresc.
f
93
spon - de var - car di Sti - ge l'on - de,
f

97
e de_l'or-ren-do Tar-ta-ro le Fu-rie su-pe-
101
rar, tut-ti quei su-pe-ra
p
104
107
re,_ tut-ti, tut-ti quei su-pe-
tr
cresc.
mf

110
rar!
Sì, tut - ti quei su - pe -
114
rar!
117
120
123

Non so più
LE NOZZE DI FIGARO

Wolfgang Amadeus Mozart
(1756 - 1791)

17
no - mi d'a-mor, di di - let - to, mi si tur - ba, mi s'al - te-ra il
crescendo
21
pet - to e a par - la - re mi sfor - za d'a -
25
mo - re un de - sì - o, un de -
29
sì - o ch'io non pos - so spie - gar, un de - sì - o,

33
un de - sì - o ch'io non pos - so spie - gar.
37
Non so più co - sa son, co - sa fac - cio, or di fo - co, o - ra so - no di
f
p
41
ghiac - cio, o - gni don - na can - giar di co - lo - re, o - gni don - na mi fa pal - pi -
f
p
45
tar, o - gni don - na mi fa pal - pi - tar, o - gni
mf
p
mf

49
don - na mi fa pal - pi - tar.
p
53
Par - lo d'a-mor ve - glian - do,
57
par - lo d'a-mor so - gnan - do, al - l'ac - qua, al - l'om - bra, ai
61
mon - ti, ai fio - ri, al - l'er - be, ai fon - ti, al - l'e - co, al - l'a - ria, ai
fp
fp

65
ven - ti, che il suon de' va - ni ac - cen - ti por - ta - no via con
f
p
crescendo
f
69
sé, por - ta - no via con sé. Par - lo d'a-mor ve -
p
74
glian - do, par - lo d'a-mor so - gnan - do, al - l'ac - qua, al -
p
78
l'om - bra, ai mon - ti, ai fio - ri, al - l'er - be, ai

† appoggiatura

Anderò, volerò, griderò
ORLANDO FINTO PAZZO

Antonio Vivaldi
(1678-1741)

8
[mf]
An-de-rò, vo-le-rò, gri-de-rò, su la Sen - na, su il Te - bro, su il
10
Re - no, vo-le-rò, gri-de-rò, gri-de - rò, ven-det - ta, bat-ta - glia, ven-det - ta, ven -
12
[f] [p] [cresc.]
det - ta, gri-de-rò, a - ni - man - do a bat - ta - glia, a ven-det - ta a bat - ta - glia, a ven -
[f] [p] [cresc.]
14
[f]
det - ta o - gni cuo - - - - - re che van - ti va-lor, a - ni -
[f]

16
man - do a bat - ta - glia, a ven-det - ta o - gni cuo - re, o - gni cuo - re che van - ti va -
18
lor.
21
[p]
Em - pio duol che mi ser - pi nel se - no,
[mf]
em - pio duol che mi ser - pi nel
Fine
[p]
[mf]
23
[f]
se - no, sca - glia, sca - glia, pur la fa - ta - le sa - et - - - -
[f]

25
ta, a fi - ni - re il mio a - cer - bo do -
27
[p]
lor. Em-pio duol che mi ser - pi nel se - no, sca-glia
[mf]
[p]
[mf]
29
[f]
pur la fa-ta - le sa-et - ta, sca-glia pur la fa-ta - le sa-et - ta, a fi -
[p]
[f]
[p]
31
[f]
D.C. al Fine
ni - re il mio a-cer - bo do - lor, a fi - ni - re il mio a-cer - bo do - lor.
D.C. al Fine
[f]

Assisa a piè d'un salice

OTELLO

Gioachino Rossini
(1792-1868)

14
tr
8va
(8)
16
tr
p
pp
20
Desdemona
con espressione
As - si - sa a piè d'un sa - li-ce, im-mer - sa nel do -
pp
24
lo - re ge - mea tra-fit - ta I-sau - ra dal più cru-de - le a -
f
28
mo - re; l'au - ra fra i ra - mi fle-bi-le ne ri-pe-te - va il
3
pp
p

32
suon.
36
I ru - scel - let - ti lim - pi - di ai
40
cal - di suoi so - spi - ri il mor - mo - rio me -
43
sce - va - no de' lor di - ver - si gi - ri;
tr
f
f

46
l'au - ra fra i ra - mi fle - bi - le ne ri - pe - te - - - va il
pp
p
49
suon.
52
pp
55
Sal - ce, d'a-mor de - li - - - zia, om - bra pie-to - sa ap-

58
pre - sta (di mie scia - gu - re im - me - mo - re) al -
61
l'ur - na mi - a fu - ne - sta, né più ri - pe - ta
64
l'au - ra de' miei la - men - ti il suon.
68
Ma stan - ca al - fin di spar - ge - re

72
me - sti so-spir - ri e pian - to, mo - rì l'af-flit - ta ver - gi - ne
76
ahi! di quel sal - ce ac-can - to! Ma stan - ca al-fin di pian - ge-re, mo -
80
rì l'af- flit - ta ver - gi-ne, mo - rì... che duol! l'in-gra-to, l'in-gra - to...
84
recitativo
Ahi-mè! che il pian-to pro-se-guir non mi fa.
Andante sostenuto
Andante sostenuto
ff recitativo
p sensibile
f

Larghetto

Deh!

Larghetto

ff p

94

cal - ma, o ciel, nel son - no per po - co le mie pe - ne;

pp *sotto voce* ff sf p *dolce*

98

fa' che l'a - ma - to be - ne mi ven - ga a con - so - lar. Se

102
poi son va - ni i prie - - ghi, di mia bre - ve ur - na in
105
se - - no di pian - to ven - ga al - me - no il ce - ne - re a ba -
pp sotto voce
ff
p
sf
109
gnar, sì, sì, il ce - ne - rè a ba - gnar.
6
3
112

Bel raggio lusinghier
SEMIRAMIDE

Gioachino Rossini
(1792-1868)

11
rà. Que - st'al - ma che si - n'or ge -
pp
14
mé, tre-mò, lan - guì... oh! co - me re-spi - rò! O - gni mio duol spa - -
ff
18
rì, spa - rì, dal cor, dal mio pen - - - - -
sf
ff
20
sier, pen - sier si di - - - le - guò il ter -
sf
pp

22
ror! Sì! Bel rag - gio lu - sin - ghier di
f
p
p
25
spe - me e di pia - cer al - fin per me bril -
simile
ff
28
lò, sì, al - fin per me bril - lò. La
pp
31
cal - ma a que - sto cor Ar -

33
sa - ce ren - de - rà. Ar -
p
35
sa - ce ri - tor - nò, qui, qui a me ver -
ff
p
38
rà,
ff
ff
41
qui ver - rà! ver - rà!
ff
pp sotto voce
ff

Allegretto
44
p

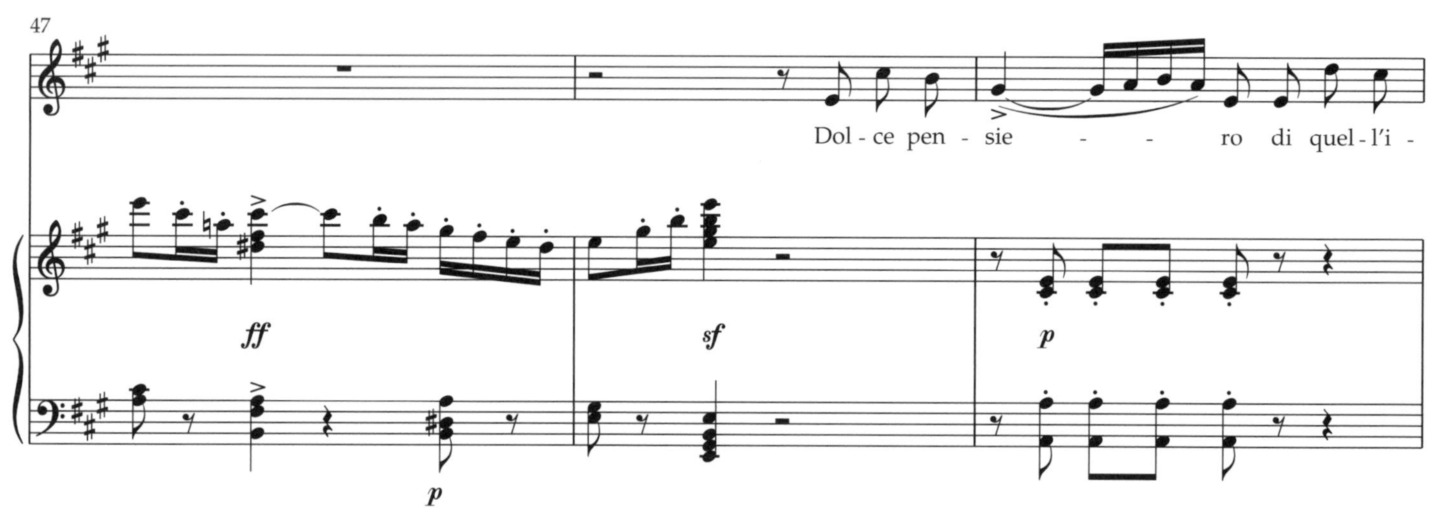
47
Dol - ce pen - sie - - ro di quel - l'i -
ff
sf
p
p

50
stan - - te, a te sor - ri - de, l'a - man - te cor, sì. Co - me più
sf

53
ca - ro, do - po il tor - men - to, è il bel mo - men - to di gio - ia e a -
p

56
mor! è il bel mo - men - - - to di
pp sotto voce
59
gio - - ia e a - mor! di gio - ia, di gio - ia e a -
62
mor! di gio - ia, di gio - ia e a -
65
mor!
Vl-

68
crescendo
70
-DE
73
f
ff
76
Ah! dol - ce pen - sie - - ro di quel - l'i -
p
79
stan - - te, a te sor - ri - de l'a - man - te cor, sì. Co - me più
sf

82
ca - ro, do - po il tor - men - to, è il bel mo - men - to di gio - ia e a -
p
85
mor! è il bel mo - men - - -
pp sotto voce
87
to di gio - - - ia e a -
89
mor! di gio - ia, di gio - ia e a -

91
mor!
di
93
gio - ia, di gio - ia e a - mor,
pp
95
di gio - ia e a -
97
mor,
di

99
gio - ia e a - mor, di gio - - ia e a - -
ff ff ff ff
f p f p f p f p
102
mor, di gio - - - ia e a - - -
ff ff ff ff
f p f p f p f p
104
mor, di gio - ia e a - mor, di gio - ia e a - -
ff
sf sf sf sf sf sf sf sf
106
mor, di gio - ia e a - mor!
sf sf sf sf

In sì barbara sciagura

SEMIRAMIDE

Gioachino Rossini
(1792-1868)

14
me - - - - - no, la - scia a te ch'io ver - - si in
16
se - - - no il mio pian - to, il mio
19
pian - - to, il mio do - lor,
21
il mio do - lor,
p

23
il mio do - lor! A que - st'a - ni - ma smar -
ff
pp
26
ri - ta, por - gi tu con - for - - to a - i - ta. Di mie
ff
29
pe - - - ne al cru - - do ec - ces - - - - - so,
pp
31
lan - gue op - pres - so, lan - gue op - pres - so in pet - to il

34
cor, lan - gue op - pres - so in pet - - - to il
36
cor, lan - - gue op - pres - - so in pet - - to il
38
cor, lan - gue op - pres - - - - - - - so in
ff
40
pet - - - - to il cor.
Allegro
Allegro
ff

8va

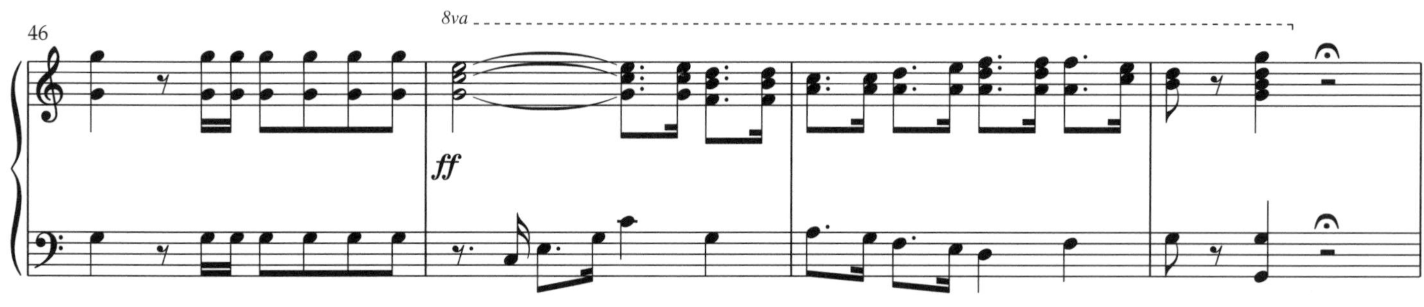
8va
ff

f
3
Sì, sì, ven - det - ta! Por - gi o - ma - i! Por - gi o -
f
ff

ma - i! Sa - cro ac-ciar del ge - - - ni - to - re, tu ri -

61
de - sti il mio va - lo - - re, già di me mag - gior mi
p
64
sen - - to. Sì, del ciel, nel fier, nel fier ci -
67
men - to, il vo - ler si com - pie - rà! Tu ri -
70
de - sti il mio va - lo - - re, già di me mag - gior mi

73
sen - - to. Sì, del ciel, nel fier, nel fier ci -
76
men - to, il vo-ler si com - pie - rà!
ff
79
Sì, sì! L'em - - pio
pp
82
dolce
ca - da! Ah!
ff
pp

85
rallentando
Ah! el - la è mia ma - dre! Al mio pian - - to for - se il
p col canto
88
pa - - dre per - do - nar - - le an - cor vor - rà, al mio
91
pian - to for - se il pa - dre per - do - nar - le an - cor vor - rà.
Allegro vivace
95
f

101
Sì, vendica -
p
simile
106
to il genitore, a lui svenato il tradi-
111
tore, pace quest'anima sperar potrà, sì,
116
sperar potra, sperar potrà.

121
Ai dolci palpiti di
8va
126
gioia e a-mo-re,
ai dolci
(8)
p
simile
131
pal-pi-ti di gio-ia e a-mo-re, fe-li-ce il
135
co-re ri-tor-ne-rà, sì, fe-li-ce il
ff

139
cor ri - - - tor - - - - ne - - -
pp
143
rà.
ff
147
f
Sì, al gran ci- men - to m'af- fret - to ar -
p
151
di - to;
ff

155
f
sì, me - co l'As - si - ria re - spi - - - re - rà.
p
ff
160
sf
dim.
166
Sì, ven - di - ca - - to il ge - ni -
p
simile
171
to - - re, a lui sve - na - to il tra - di - to - re,

176
pa - ce que - st'a - ni - ma spe - rar po - trà, sì, spe - rar po -
181
trà, spe - rar po - trà. Ai
186
dol - ci pal - pi - ti di gio - ia e a -
191
mo - re, ai dol - ci
simile

195
pal - - pi - ti di gio - ia e a - mo - - - - re, fe - li - ce il
199
co - re ri - tor - ne - rà, sì, fe - li - ce il cor
ff
pp
204
ri - - - tor - - - ne - - - rà,
ff
208
f
ri - tor - ne - rà,
ri - tor - ne - rà,
8va

212
ri - - - tor - - - - ne - - - - rà,
(8)
216
f
ri - tor - ne - rà,
ri - tor - ne - rà,
(8)
220
ri - - - tor - - - - ne - - - - rà,
(8)
sf
sf
224
ri - tor - ne - rà, ri -
sf

229
tor - ne - rà, ri - tor - ne - rà, ri -
sf sf sf sf
234
tor - ne - rà, ri - tor - ne - rà.
3
238
243

Di tanti palpiti

TANCREDI

Gioachino Rossini
(1792-1868)

16

20
Tancredi *recitativo*
Oh pa-tria! dol-ce, e in-gra-ta pa-tria! al-fi-ne a te ri-tor-no! Io ti sa-
recitativo
p

25
lu-to, o ca-ra ter-ra de-gli a-vi mie-i: ti ba-cio. È que-sto per me gior-no se-

30
re-no: co-min-cia il cor a re-spi-rar-mi in se-no.
Allegro
tr
Allegro
f
sf
p

35
A-me-na-i-de!
o mio pen-sier so -
41
a - ve, so - lo de' miei so-spir, de' vo-ti mie-i ce-les-te og-get-to,
ff
45
io ven-ni al-fin: io vo-glio, sfi-dan-do il mio de -
f
49
sti - no, qual-un-que si - a, me-ri - tar - ti, o pe-rir, a - ni-ma mi - a.
p

Maestoso
Tu che ac-cen - di que - sto co - - - re, tu che
Maestoso
pp
f
des - ti il va - lor mi - - - o, al - ma glo - ria, dol - - ce a -
mo - re, se - con - da - te il bel de - sì - o, ca - da un
a piacere
em - - - pio tra - - - di - to - re, co - ro - na - te la mia fé.
ff sf sf sf sf sf sf col canto f a tempo

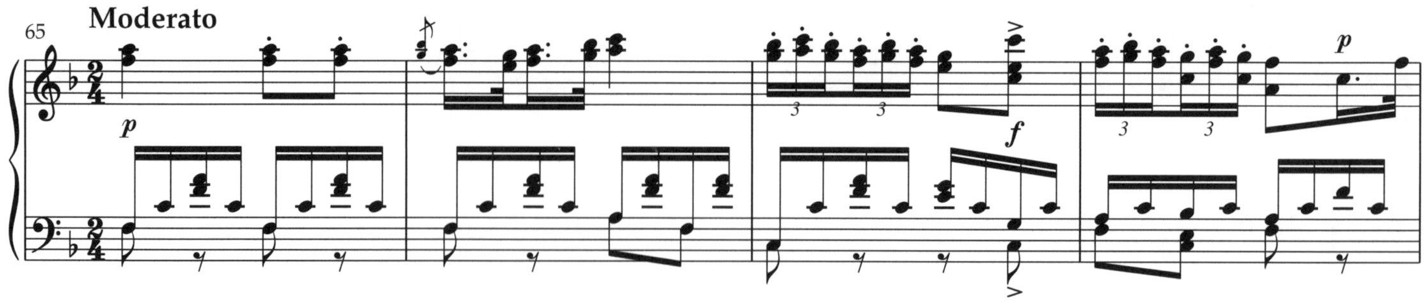
65
Moderato
p
f
p

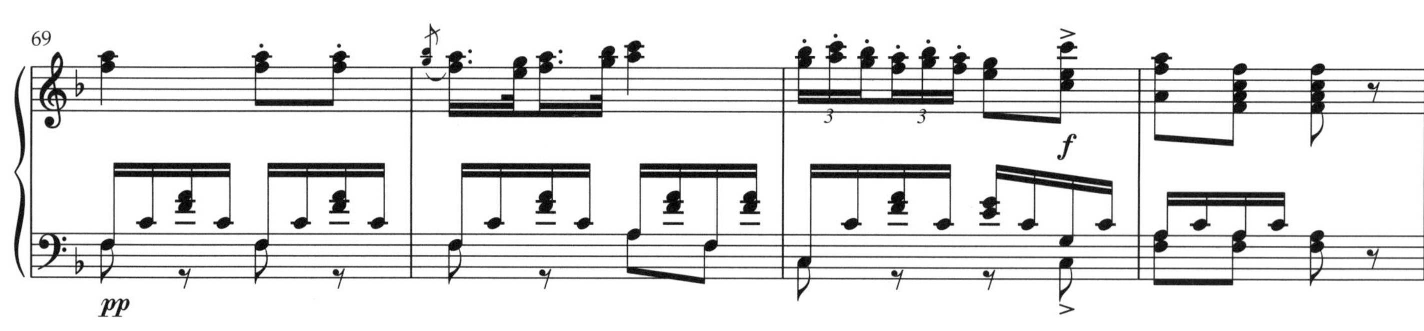
69
pp
f

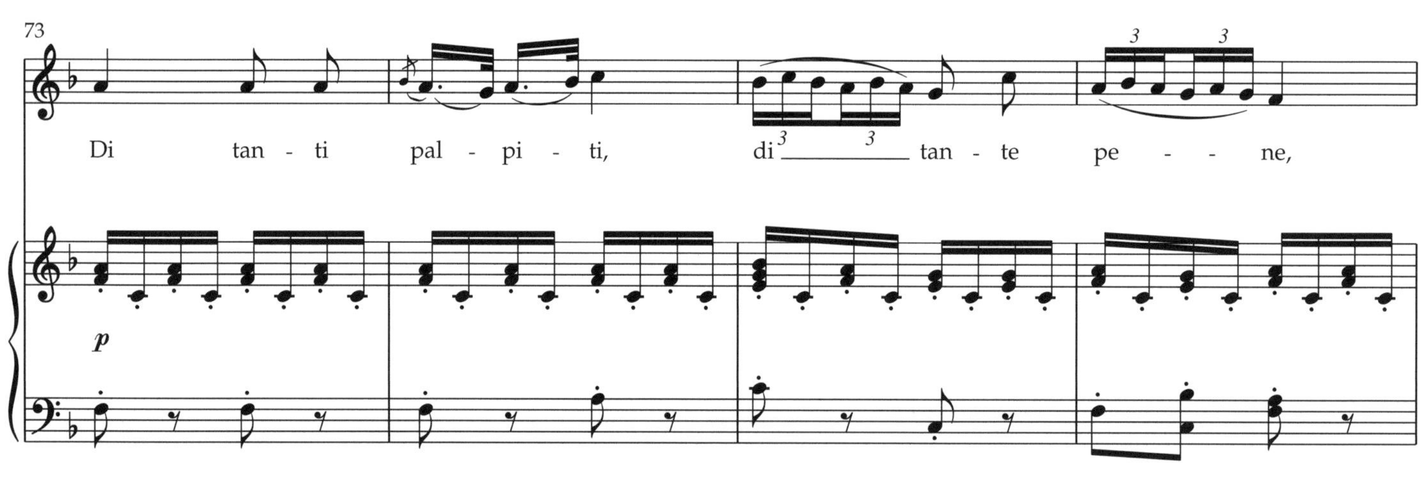
73
Di tan - ti pal - pi - ti, di tan - te pe - - - ne,
p

77
da te mio be - - - ne, spe - - ro mer - cé.

81
Mi ri - ve - dra - i... ti ri - ve - drò...
85
ti ri - ve - drò...
p
pp
89
ne' tuoi bei rai mi pa - sce - rò. De -
3
3
93
li - - ri, so - spi - - ri, ac - cen - - ti, con -
p

96
ten - - ti!... De - li - ri, so - spi - ri, ac -
crescendo
rinforz.
99
cen - ti, con - ten - ti! Sa - - rà fe -
f
sf
p
102
li - - ce, il 3 3 cor mel di - - ce,
3 3
105
il mio de - sti - no vi - ci 3 3 - no a te.

109
Mi ri - ve - dra - i... ti ri - ve - drò...
113
ti ri - ve - drò...
pp
117
ne' tuoi bei rai mi pa - sce -
120
rò, mi ri - ve - dra - i, ti ri - ve - drò, ne' tuoi bei ra - i mi pa - sce -
pp
3

124
rò, mi ri - ve - dra - i, ti _ ri - ve - drò, ne'tuoi bei ra - i mi pa-sce -

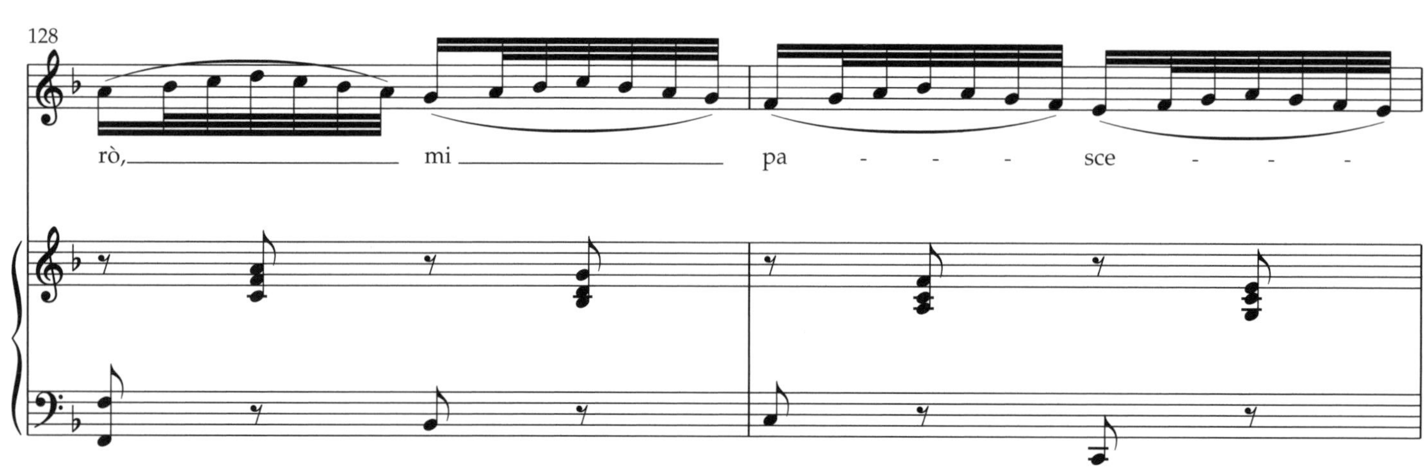
128
rò, mi pa - - - - sce - - - -

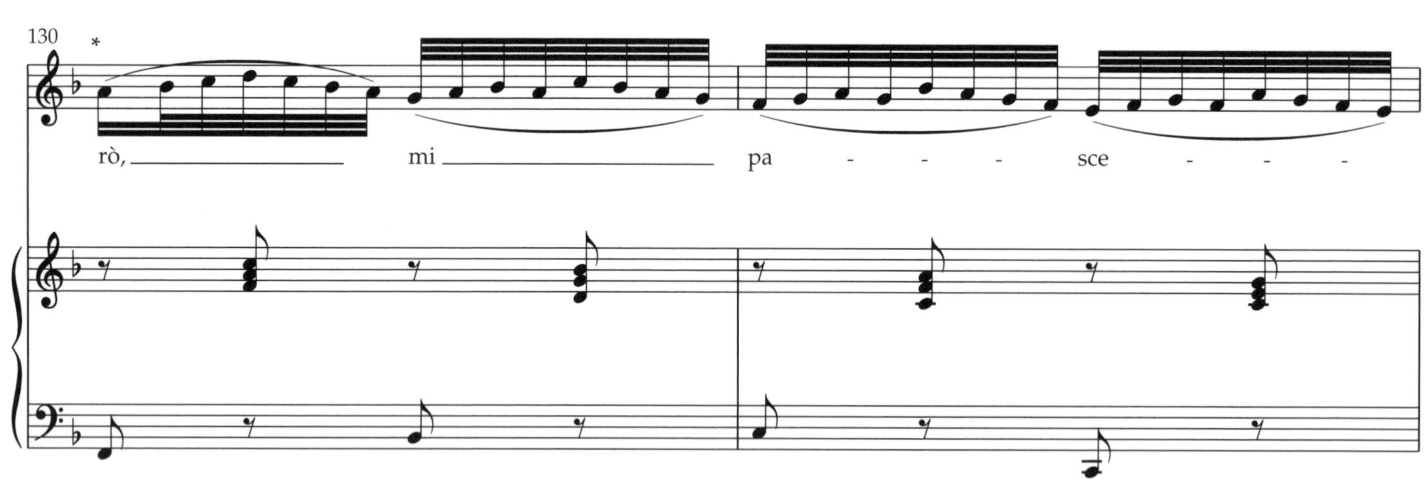
130
*
rò, mi pa - - - - sce - - - -

* Varianti di Rossini
1
2

132
rò, ne' tuoi bei ra - i mi pa - sce -
f
f
f
f
134
rò, ne' tuoi bei rai mi pa - sce -
f
136
rò, mi pa - sce - rò, mi pa - sce -
139
rò, mi pa - sce - rò.

Stride la vampa

IL TROVATORE

Giuseppe Verdi
(1813-1901)

31
don - - na s'a - van - za; si - ni - stra splen -
38
de sui vol - ti or - ri - - bi - li la te - tra
45
fiam - - ma che s'al - za, che s'al - za al ciel,
51
che s'al - za al ciel!

58
ff
65
Stri - - de la vam - - pa! Giun - - ge la vit - - ti -
pp
72
ma ne - - ro ve - sti - - - ta, di - - scin - ta e
79
scal - - za; gri - - do fe - ro - - ce di
f
marcato
pp
pp

86
f
mor - te le - va - si; l'e - - co il ri - pe - te di
marcato
[pp]
94
tr
bal - za in bal - za; si - ni - stra splen - de sui
102
vol - ti or - ri - bi - li la te - tra fiam - ma che s'al - za, che
110
s'al - za al ciel, che s'al - za al ciel!
ff

Condotta ell'era in ceppi

IL TROVATORE

Giuseppe Verdi
(1813-1901)

13
f
p
ta - - - i, ma in-va-no a-prir - - - mi... in-van ten-tò la
16
dim.
mi - - se-ra fer - mar - si e be-ne-dir - - - mi!
dim.
19
Ché, fra be-stem-mie o-sce - - - - ne, pun - gen - - - do - la coi
p
22
f
fer - ri, al ro - go la cac - - cia-va-no gli scel-le-ra-ti sgher - ri!
pp
pp

25
Al - lor, con tron-co ac-cen - - - - to, "Mi
28
ven - - di - ca!" scla - mò... Quel det - - to un e - - - co e -
31
ter - - no in que-sto cor, in que-sto cor la - sciò.
34
Il fi - glio giun - si a ra - pir del Con - te; lo tra - sci - nai qui

36
me - co... le fiam-me ar-dean già pron - te.
f
p
f
p
f
p
39
Ei di-strug-ge - a-si in pian - - - to...
io mi sen - ti - va il
pp
42
Allegretto (♩. = 60)
co - - re di - la - nia - to, in - fran-to!
Allegretto (♩. = 60)
ppp
47
sotto voce e declamato
Quan-d'ec - co a - gli e - gri spir - ti,
ppp
co - me in un
tr
pp
sotto voce
tr

53
so - - gno, ap - par - ve la vi -
tr
57
sion fe - ra - le di spa - ven - to - - - se
tr
tr
62
lar - ve! Gli sgher-ri! ed il sup - pli - zio!...
tr
67
la ma - dre smor - ta in vol - to... scal - za,

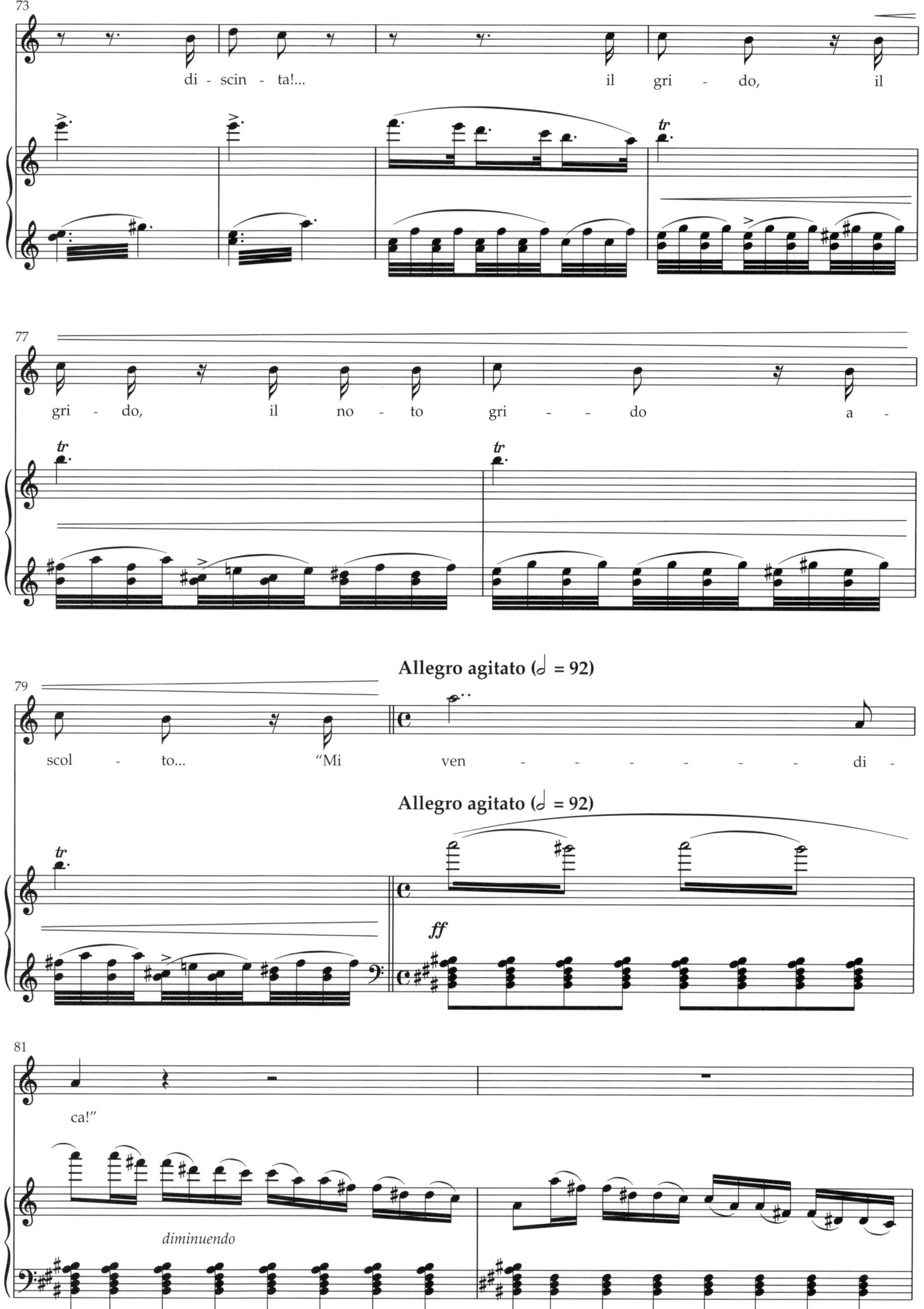
73
di - scin - ta!...
il gri - do, il
77
gri - do, il no - to gri - - do a -
79
Allegro agitato (𝅗𝅥 = 92)
scol - to... "Mi ven - - - - - - - di -
Allegro agitato (𝅗𝅥 = 92)
ff
81
ca!"
diminuendo

83
pp agitatissimo declamato
La ma - no con - vul - sa
pp
86
ten - do... strin - go la vit - ti - ma... nel fo - co la
90
trag - go, la so - spin - go!...
ff
93
Ces - sa il fa - tal de - li - rio...
pp
pp

95
l'or - ri - da sce - - - na fug - ge... la
ff
97
fiam - - ma sol di - vam - pa, e la sua pre - da
pp
100
strug - ge! Pur vol - go in - tor - no il guar - do, e in - nan - zi a me veg -
ff
pp
p
104
g'i - o del - l'em - pio Con - - te il fi - glio! Il fi - glio

108
mi - o, mio fi - glio a - vea bru - cia - - - - to!
ff
111
Ah!
113
Mio
115
straziante
fi - glio! mio fi - glio! il fi - glio
fff

118
mi - - o! il fi - glio mi - - - - o a - vea bru -
122
cia - to!
124
dim.
126
pp
sempre dim.

128
130
Sul ca - po mi - - o le
pp
134
allarg. poco a poco
chio - - me sen - to driz - zar - - si an - cor, driz -
allarg. poco a poco
139
morendo
zar - si an - cor, driz - zar - si an - cor!
ancora allarg. e morendo
ppp
pp